Praise from readers of the first editio and *Freelancing*:

'I'm about to leave my company and become a consultant (of the passionate practitioner variety). It's been a long time coming, and now feels like the right time . . . but, naturally, such a big decision has not been achieved without a lot of soul searching . . . and attendant fear. I decided finally to do it about two weeks ago, then started scouting around for books to read. Yours was the first one I came across in a bookshop in Wellington. I doubt whether I'll bother to look for more . . . it seemed to anticipate all my worries and provide sensible practical responses.'
—*Bronwyn Sterling, Wellington, New Zealand*

'Thanks to your book I have a clear idea of everything I need to do to get my business up and running . . . Your book saved me six months of trying to figure out what I needed to do.'
—*Dr Ingrid Baade, Consultant Statistician, Brisbane*

'I received the book last week after having previously borrowed it from the library. I have now read it for the second time; it is plastered with post it notes! I recommended it to a colleague the other day and will continue recommending it.'
—*Elizabeth Devine, Devine Law At Work, Sydney*

'I bought your book the day I went into the Smartlicence office to register my name. I was still working full time at that stage and working for myself was only a dream but registering the name was the first step.

I went home and got stuck into your book and after a week started talking and planning about my business and securing my first contract. Four weeks later I became a consultant and I love it. Now, three years later, I still love it and am seriously focused on expanding the business beyond myself.

Just wanted to let you know that if I had not have picked up your book that day I'd probably be frustrated and not enjoying the freedom and strength that being a consultant provides.'
—*Sarah Sheppard, My Marketing Manager, Toowong, Queensland*

'Great book. Got it last week and I have completed it already. Completed my business plan with the assistance of your book. Lots of good stuff . . . Thanks for the great information.'
—*John Duffield, UMACS Business Solutions, Brunswick, Victoria*

'You should feel very proud of your book—it's inspiring without being too starry-eyed, and amusing to boot.'
—*Alison Hallahan, Capital Foresight Pty Ltd, Fitzroy, Victoria*

'I heard about you through your book which is in the Graduate School of Business (University of Cape Town) library. My area of "specialisation" has needed a boost and your book is helping me refine my thinking and where my real talents lie.'
—*Pam Moore, Cape Town, South Africa*

'I purchased your book two months before I started my business and found it extremely useful. It is full of practical and pragmatic advice and now after two years I still refer back to my copy regularly. I used the proposal example for my first tender application and was successful. I still use it to this day and have a better than seventy per cent success rate!'
—*Gary McMahon, Dunsborough, Western Australia*

'Your book is fantastic and I am already 2/3 of the way through it. The marketing chapter was particularly useful as it is the area I struggle with. Having spent 31 years in the army you don't have to worry about marketing! We don't really "sell" our services in Defence; we just do what we are told.'
—*Zac Zaharias, Director, Peak Learning, Canberra*

'As a career coach working with many people who are looking to use their skills in the consulting or contracting arena, I have found Ian's book *Consulting, Contracting and Freelancing* to be an absolute gem. It addresses so many questions and backs up the answers with very practical and relevant examples.'
—*John Link, Richardson Recruitment, Newcastle*

'Early in my career as a freelancer, I bought one book—Ian Benjamin's *Consulting, Contracting and Freelancing*. This book is practical: it gives advice you can get on with. It's realistic: it doesn't make pie-in-the-sky promises. And, it's well-informed— by Ian's and others' experiences. For these reasons, I've returned to the book again and again.'
—*Chris Walker, Writer and Editor, Perth*

'As a freelance journalist and publisher of an online magazine devoted to small and internet business, I read many business books. This one is distinctive as being truly practical and inspirational. It really does detail a path to freelance success.'
—*Susan Kirk, journalist, LingoWritingStudio www.lingo.net.au, Wellington Point, Queensland*

CONSULTING, CONTRACTING AND FREELANCING

CONSULTING, CONTRACTING AND FREELANCING

BE YOUR OWN BOSS

Second edition

IAN BENJAMIN

ALLEN&UNWIN

This edition first published in 2007

Allen & Unwin
83 Alexander Street
Crows Nest NSW 2065
Australia
Phone: (61 2) 8425 0100
Fax: (61 2) 9906 2218
Email: info@allenandunwin.com
Web: http://www.allenandunwin.com

National Library of Australia
Cataloguing-in-Publication entry:

Benjamin, Ian.
    Consulting, contracting and freelancing : be your own boss.

    2nd ed.
    Includes index.
    ISBN 978 1 74175 297 7 (pbk.).

    1. Consultants. 2. Self-employed. 3. Letting of contracts.
    I. Title.

658.1141

Set in 11/13 pt ACaslon Regular by Midland Typesetters, Australia

10 9 8 7 6 5 4 3 2 1

For my father
Vernon Alfred Henry Benjamin, 1914–2001

Survivor of the Burma Railroad, Changi, Japan coal mines
Man of the land and people
Family man
Wise man of abundant common sense

CONTENTS

PREFACE

Until I became a consultant in 1987, I had worked for eleven companies or organisations in the seventeen years since I had left university with my degree in economics and later, a diploma in education. My longest-held job lasted three and a half years, the shortest five weeks. In each job I started keenly and worked hard. I was often rewarded, but I was rarely afforded the independence and freedom that I envied in those of my friends who were self-employed. They followed a range of activities—a printer, a lawyer, a builder. I also met many independent investors in my years in the finance sector. I wanted to work for myself too, but I just wasn't quite sure what activity to pursue.

My first attempt at self-employment in 1985 was as a financial planner, a job which I coupled with finance broking. I had been in business for only five weeks when I was offered a job in a merchant bank too good to turn down. Two years into that job, one of the clients of the bank, whose company was to be floated on the stock exchange, offered me a position on his board. I resigned from the bank, and the stock market collapsed one week later, on 18 October 1987. A few weeks into my new job I disagreed with my new employer about what to do with the company's assets in the wake of the stock market crash, and left that job too.

Within a week of leaving I had done my first consultancy, earned $1500, and saw prosperity beckoning. Two weeks later I had another $1000 . . . I was on my way to successful self-employment! It was to be four months before I earned another fee.

Soon afterwards I was offered a permanent job with the Australian Merchant Bankers Association, but it required relocating to Sydney, a move which did not suit my wife. AMBA and I came to an arrangement whereby I would work as a contractor while also pursuing my own consulting activities. That provided an excellent transition into successful self-employment.

Since then I have undertaken over 2000 short-term engagements as a trainer, facilitator and speaker. While most of these have been here at home in Australia, I have also had 30 trips to work for clients in Singapore, Hong Kong and New Zealand. There is continuous inter-state travel, as my main strategy has been to run seminars in the four main eastern cities, taking advantage of the local opportunities that have arisen from them.

Along the way I have made many good relationships, foremost among them with Sydney careers adviser and counsellor Mary Anthony. Mary came to a 'How to be a Successful Consultant' seminar in Sydney in 1994, and again three years later, when it was time for her to make the move into self-employment. She has referred many aspiring consultants to these workshops, and I in turn have often sought clarity, advice and comfort in her words of wisdom.

About six years ago a young manager in AMP asked me if I would be his mentor. I didn't know what to say! Although flattered I un-graciously declined, recommending that he appoint someone who knew how to achieve long-term goals within large organisations.

The young man is Andrew Crawford. He has developed his career and achieved significant results. I thank him for his continuing support, leadership and promotion of my services in a number of places. Andrew is one of the most authentic leaders of the hundreds with whom I have worked.

I have enjoyed long conversations over many years with the follow-ing consultants, who are friends and in some instances associates: Glenda May, Deb Fullwood, Frank Kelloway, Jim Longworth, Bill

Synnot, Helen Fletcher, Larry Watson and Kevin Reid. I foresee that my recent involvement with the Australasian Facilitators' Network will add others to this list.

There are a number of longer term clients who have become confidants and I have great respect for them and their leadership skills. I mention them in appreciation of their support, engagement and continued advocacy of my services for more than five years in each case.

Randal Dennings of Clayton Utz in Brisbane and Sydney who launched the first edition of this book at Riverbend Books in Bulimba, Brisbane in August 2003.

In Sydney, Andrew Crawford of Suncorp and Dr Charlotte Hespe of the Sydney Institute of General Practice Education and Training.

In Canberra, Andrew Balmaks and his partners, Peter Murphy and Rick Vickers, of Noetic Solutions Pty Ltd; Peter Bell, Jenifer Fredericks and Rex Waite of Alliance Consulting Group and Dr Lyndal Thorburn of Innovation Dynamics.

In Melbourne, Keith James of Hall & Wilcox, Chris Johnston of Context Pty Ltd and Joe Librandi, formerly of CPA Australia.

I also acknowledge the leadership teams of CPA Australia and Pitcher Partners. I have many clients that I have worked for on an irregular basis over many years and am grateful for their continuing support.

I thank Geelong accountant Roger Holding for his technical advice in both editions.

For her encouragement and insistence that I write this book, I thank Tonya Jennings. Tonya now has her own business at http://www.ontheridge.com.au.

I also thank my children, Eliza and Will, who mailed out thousands of newsletters in the pre-Internet era. They also knew when to be quiet when I was speaking on the 'business' phone at home and they provided lots of ideas for my presentations and suggestions about how I conduct myself.

Eliza often proofreads my work and provides reality checks. Will, in his quiet engaging manner, reminds me of my youth and gives me perspective on what is important. We have shared many memorable dinners including some in Maroochydore, Broome and St Kilda. Long may it continue.

In 2003 my partner and I moved to the hinterland overlooking Maroochydore on Queensland's Sunshine Coast. As I don't have a job that gives me postings in beautiful and interesting places, I have done it myself. Here in south-east Queensland, I find this business model that you are about to discover works well.

Read on and, if you are interested, why not do your own thing too?

Readers are invited to visit <http://www.ianbenjamin.com.au> for any dialogue.

Ian Benjamin
2007

1
WHY BECOME A CONSULTANT?

We have two choices. We can make a living, or we can design a life.

Jim Rohn[1]

In what job can you arrive at the office within a minute of leaving home, park your car only metres away, enjoy immediate access to your boss, determine when you start and finish, pursue your passion—what you are good at—and sometimes earn in one day what you used to take a week to earn? Oh, and by the way, there are minimal office politics.

This book is about more than having a job. It is about lifestyle. Practising as a consultant—by doing independent contracting, freelancing or consulting—can be a gateway to living the life you want, doing the work you want, ideally for the clients you want, and possibly from the place you want.

As a consultant the benefits you stand to gain are very specific. You will be able to:

- Work from home—and this will be pure delight for many. There are times when you will work extremely long days but you will be able to go for a walk just after lunch or at 4 pm. You can return to your desk without travel and for just an hour. You will be on the way to balancing home and work life.

1

- Work hard and fast and make lots of money; or implement that plan of yours to work not quite so hard and to pursue your hobby, to spend more hours each week and year in your garden, on the golf course, travelling the country and the world, learning a language, flying an aircraft, diving under the sea, helping others and reading books. Get to know your children, do more active parenting. Get to know your own family. You will be further along the road to balance.
- Do the type of work you enjoy and be more focused on the tasks you thrive on, rather than spending much of your time dealing with internal political issues.
- Enjoy variation in your work and in the way your days are spent. Instead of working with one organisation, you will experience the stimulation of working with many, and learning more about people and where they work. You also learn more about the practice of your craft as you see it applied in a variety of situations and industries. Travel is often required, so you learn about places as well.
- Exercise control over your fate. You choose what you want to do. You plan for the risks of self-employment and manage those risks. Downsizing and restructuring will be issues at the margin of your business rather than at the core of your life.
- Use only minimal capital to set up your business. You will need access to funds, however, to get you through the set-up phase, which for most people is from six to nine months.
- Choose where to live. Subject to the needs of those with whom you live, this might be the golden opportunity to leave the capital cities and go somewhere warmer, somewhere more serene and somewhere that costs less to enjoy.
- Keep working. Don't retire—you possess a lot of useful information, and there are many people and organisations that can benefit from what you know. We are a long time dead, and it is generally accepted that we are a long time retired. Stay active and be paid for your contributions.

WHAT ARE CONSULTING, CONTRACTING AND FREELANCING?

Practitioners of these occupations are identified by several common characteristics. They:

- possess specialist skills;
- are extensively experienced in some areas;
- possess specialist knowledge;
- work for a number of clients on an irregular basis;
- are self-employed; and
- maintain an office of their own—often at home.

Queenslanders pack their clothes in a port while the rest of Australia uses a suitcase. Beer drinkers in New South Wales ask for a middy; Victorians order a pot. These examples of different names given to the same object to some extent reflect what happens with the words consulting, contracting and freelancing, although in this case the basis for distinction tends to be industrial rather than geographical.

Each of these three activities involves a person with a particular skill set and knowledge base working on an occasional basis for one or a number of clients. In certain industries, including the engineering, construction and manufacturing industries, the terms 'consulting' and 'contracting' are used extensively. The term 'freelancing' is used more extensively in publishing, broadcasting, the arts, advertising and marketing. Freelancing is also the vernacular expression for someone doing occasional work here and there, while consulting and contracting tend to be used in a more formal context.

Some observers see consultants as adopting a higher profile position than contractors or freelancers. However, it really depends upon the industry. In activities associated with the creative arts, leading performers and practitioners are usually described as freelancers, while those who advise the organisations on issues related to management, technical aspects of production and marketing are called consultants.

In this book I use the words 'consulting' and 'freelancing' interchangeably. A useful distinction can, however, be made between these terms and 'contracting'. In his book *Flawless Consulting*, Peter Block defines consulting as 'setting the parameters' whereas contracting is working 'within the parameters'.[2] When consultants start a project, they have a problem or a blank sheet of paper before them. When contractors start a project, they have a series of steps before them. The consultant works out what is to be done, then the contractor does it. It is often the case that the one person performs both functions.

Consultants and freelancers tend to differentiate themselves according to the methodology they use, their approach and their reputation, factors that collectively contribute some form of uniqueness. The marketing programs of the consultant and freelancer are directed towards establishing their name as a brand that has unique features. The uniqueness allows them to have greater flexibility in setting the price of their services.

By contrast, contractors market themselves as experts in certain established methodologies and as being able to deliver a uniform quality within a specified time frame. This is all done within a relatively narrow price band. It is often said that contractors are *price takers* whereas consultants are *price makers*.

In the first edition of this book, I used the term 'solo service professional' to include consultants, contractors and freelancers. In this edition, I use the term 'consultant' to describe all three. Where special comment is appropriate, I will use the terms contracting and freelancing.

WHAT DO YOU NEED TO BECOME A CONSULTANT?

Whether you are a consultant, freelancer or contractor, the key ingredients in establishing yourself as a consultant are:

- **A strong desire** to create a lifestyle giving you optimal flexibility, control and variety. For many, this is the major benefit in becoming a consultant. Self-employment can suit you if you have young children to raise, you want balance in your life and you have other interests you wish to pursue. It also gives you greater control over your life. You can plan and act to get the type of work you want and the type of clients that you prefer.

- **A range of specialist skills and knowledge,** acquired over a number of years, that you can apply for the benefit of clients. If you analyse them, you will be able to package them as groups of skills applicable in a variety of situations. It is better to think of them in terms of the benefits they give to clients than in terms of the technical aspects which interest you and other providers of the services. Freelance photographers, for example, may talk of shutter speeds, aperture openings and placement of lights, but their clients will be more interested in looking good, feeling great and having tangible records of happy events.

- **A capacity to communicate** with prospective clients about their needs. This involves giving the clients reasons to have confidence in you, demonstrating empathy and understanding of their situation, using their language in their context, and avoiding giving them stock standard solutions to problems they don't have.

- **A persistent attitude.** Making sufficient approaches to a broad range of prospective clients. It is usually necessary to make many approaches to gain one engagement. This process must be multiplied, because you will need many engagements. When you start making direct approaches the odds of success may seem to resemble the long shots in the Melbourne Cup, but the odds improve with experience and with practice. The reasons for non-engagement will be reasonable in most cases, mostly relating to inappropriate timing, a perceived lack of need or an apparent lack of comfort on the client's part with some aspect of your overall approach. Even when the reason for rejection isn't fair it's all still part of life, and so you learn a little, look for the next opportunity and learn a little more. If you go for too long without success, you should seek advice, take action and try again.

- **Being a risk taker.** There is an entrepreneurial aspect to becoming a consultant. First, you need to create circumstances where potential clients are aware that you are available for hire and then to be able to negotiate a contract with your hirer. Then you need to deliver on your promise—to provide the appropriate service and result. The rewards for taking and successfully managing this risk are described at the start of this chapter. To some people, this risk is really a series of exciting opportunities to do interesting and rewarding work on a discrete assignment basis for which you are reasonably well rewarded.

BEING A SERVICE PROVIDER IS NOT ENOUGH!

Freelancers, consultants and contractors are all service providers. So too are all the occupations listed in the *Yellow Pages*. Service providers give clients what they ask for. They take orders and in doing so address the expressed wants of clients.

Contractors are usually given a full description of the outcome desired by the client, and perhaps the steps or methodology necessary to achieve the outcome. It is the client who defines what is to be done and how it will be done. For example, a client may request that the book-keeper use a particular system, rather than just coming up with the necessary reports.

Consultants, however, may often be dealing with a client who is not aware of the nature and extent of the problem and really has no idea about the solution, very often because they lack knowledge of the particular area: some clients may mistakenly request an inappropriate service delivery, or define key words or processes differently from the service provider's understanding. Either way, it is vital that service providers ask searching questions of their clients to define the real need and to confirm that their engagement will solve the problem.

The primary diagnostic tool that consultants use to uncover a client's real need is the question. Contractors who ask too many questions, on the other hand, may well be viewed as out of line and not suitable for the task because they are behaving inconsistently with the client's expectations.

When you start your business you will have the objective of doing good work so that your good name will spread and the phone will keep ringing with offers of engagement. For this to happen, it is imperative that you have a clear understanding of what is required of you as the service provider.

DEFINE THE SERVICE REQUIRED

A Brisbane-based training consultant delivered a workshop entitled 'Leadership Skills' to a public sector client in Sydney. Four months later the consultant sent out a newsletter to all her clients. It featured information about a new workshop called 'Advanced Leadership Skills'. Subsequently, the PA to the public sector client in Sydney rang to request delivery of the 'Advanced Leadership Skills' workshop to 100 people within the organisation.

Five days prior to the scheduled workshop, the consultant rang the client to confirm the number of attendees. Yes, it was still 100. Further questioning revealed that none of these people had attended her basic 'Leadership Skills' workshop, nor had they had any other leadership skills training.

At this stage it became apparent that the client thought he was ordering the original workshop that the consultant had delivered. He had not registered that there were two levels of workshop, having jumped to a conclusion on seeing the name of the trainer and the words 'Leadership Skills'. Consultant and client quickly sorted out the misunderstanding and the consultant brought the appropriate workshop manuals and materials to Sydney.

There was some initial confusion in the first few minutes of the workshop as the training consultant explained to the attendees that the workshop was properly called 'Leadership Skills' and that it was the appropriate workshop for the situation. The body language of some of the attendees suggested they were unhappy at finding themselves attending a lesser version of the workshop they had expected, but fortunately their antagonism soon dissipated as they moved into the subject and their first activity of the morning.

As shown here, being merely a service provider runs a high risk of inappropriate service delivery. A client's understanding of the service to be delivered may be quite different from the provider's understanding of what is to be delivered. This mismatch is due solely to a lack of appropriate communication. As service providers are the subject experts, it is reasonable that they take responsibility for the outcome.

An analogous situation would be for a patient complaining of a stomach ache to request a surgeon to perform an appendectomy. A doctor who did this with no further diagnosis would be simply taking orders and providing the service—being merely a service provider and no more.

HOW DOES CONSULTING DIFFER FROM BEING AN EMPLOYEE?

A survey conducted by *Business Review Weekly* reported that the main benefit recognised by the newly self-employed is in the area of independence and freedom[3]—the freedom to pursue their own vision, to do the work they like and in their preferred situation, be it location or industry, and to do so with their preferred clients.

These factors combine to give a high level of job satisfaction which may compensate for the irregularity and sometimes reduced level of income that self-employed consultants experience.

The major concern for the same group was the accompanying lack of financial security. Most consultants start out with one or two clients in mind, but building their client base beyond that point is an unknown factor. However, the completion of these first assignments creates a track record for the fledgling consultant. The transition to the next stage becomes much easier when the consultant can reflect the confidence gained from having successfully completed a few commercial projects, and has independent third-party endorsement from satisfied clients.

There are differing perceptions as to how consultants and employees view their obligations. Most consultants would argue that they are only as good as their last job and that their reputation is on the line all the time. They therefore display a high level of obligation and responsibility to perform the task to the best of their ability. Often their time is recorded and the client is required to pay only for work done. The employee perception is that they sometimes find consultants to be self-interested, that they overcharge and that they are always looking for the next engagement. It is relatively easy to find evidence where these conflicting perceptions both approximate reality.

The same article listed four things that former corporate executives miss as consultants: the thrill of putting deals together; using the skills they had spent a career developing; the social contact of the office; and being in the loop. My comment is that the first two of these aspects can be part of your consultancy career if you want them to be. You become the deal facilitator and you continue to use your deal-making skills.

HOW IS BEING A CONSULTANT DIFFERENT FROM BUYING A BUSINESS?

The main difference here is that the capital requirements for setting up your own consultancy are minimal whereas it requires a considerable sum to purchase a business that will pay a regular income. Most good business opportunities are quite costly, with the purchaser paying a multiple of the earnings as the acquisition price. If the business were to generate an income of say $60 000 and the industry generally accepted a multiple of 3 as the acquisition price (purchase price = 3 × annual earnings), the purchase price would be $180 000. One often hears of multiples of 10 or 15 × earnings, which in the case of $60 000 would see a purchase price of $600 000 or $900 000. Management rights on apartment buildings are often quoted at 8 × earnings. (In theory, this means that the investment pays for itself in eight years.)

Another difference is that the operating costs in consultancies are relatively low, while retail businesses may carry stock and debtors of considerable magnitude.[4]

The major asset of any consultancy business is the skill, knowledge and business contacts of the owner. These are difficult to pass on to others so very few consultant businesses are sold. Sales are more common where there is a group of partners and a newcomer can acquire equity in an existing business. In this case they will also gain a share of the profits and have something to sell when they in turn retire.

The major benefit of purchasing a business is that one is purchasing an income stream. Great care and diligence need to be exercised in these situations, as the stakes are high, the sums large and the possibility of recovery from an adverse situation relatively small.

CHECK ALL CLAIMS BEFORE YOU BUY

Adelaide-based consultant Christine saw an advertisement for the sale of consultancy licences for a strategic planning and business process re-engineering service that could be offered to small business. A reliable income level was assured, with examples of others who had bought these franchises.

Support was provided in the form of training and of marketing materials, including scripts of what to say to prospective clients. The only aspect missing was customers. To obtain these, Christine was to go through the *Yellow Pages* and randomly choose businesses to approach. This was pure cold calling.

One year later, Christine was $50 000 poorer and emotionally deflated. She had suffered continuous rejection for twelve months. Christine was offering a service about which all she knew was what she had learned in one week's training and any subsequent reading. The deeper she got into the subject area, the more she realised the less she knew. Her confidence was further eroded when the franchisor resumed advertising, offering further franchises for sale in what she thought was her sole area.

It is easier to be successful if you stay in an area of activity where you have relevant experience, if you offer your services into industries that you know, into geographical areas you know and to people who know of you. Any business requiring pure cold calling will want to have a very observable benefit. Services, being intangible, often look overpriced and unenticing.

WHY IS CONSULTING A GROWTH INDUSTRY?

The number of consultants has increased rapidly in recent years. The Melbourne *Age* reported that the home-based sector had been growing at 16 per cent in the past two years and that Australian Bureau of Statistics figures reveal that there are more than 770 000 home-based businesses in Australia. There are a number of reasons for this.

Since the mid 1980s organisations have become more focused on their core business. They have continually retrenched staff considered non-essential to the business. Many of the people let go have been those with extensive knowledge of the organisation, its client base, its stakeholders and its processes. Although they were often the more experienced employees, they had to go as they cost more each week with their higher salaries. Some of them were also more resistant to change. Much of this downsizing activity was undertaken when there were strong commercial pressures on organisations to reduce costs. As the economy picked up and new opportunities presented themselves in the marketplace, businesses and government departments found they needed to hire outsiders, consultants, if they wished to take advantage of these opportunities.

There are many other reasons why consultants are in demand. Business processes are developing rapidly and it is difficult for managers in organisations to keep up to date as well as to meet production targets, budgets and other internal performance criteria. Management is increasingly involved with management *per se* and finding that it needs to rely on outsiders for the latest technical advice.

While many large entities have a preference for engaging internationally renowned consulting firms, among SMEs (small- to medium-sized enterprises) and in specialised areas within larger corporations and government departments there is extensive use of smaller firms and consultants who are ideally placed to provide advice.[5]

In like manner, senior managers often feel isolated within their organisation. They feel pressure from above and below to be seen to be competent. Many managers look to develop relationships with consultants so they can be briefed from time to time, not only to find out what is in the marketplace, but also to bounce ideas around and validate the decisions they are about to make. Experienced consultants are aware of this and work hard to cultivate client relationships based on trust and the provision of utility to those clients. I have often observed that consultants who don't succeed in their own businesses have failed to make these sorts of connections.

On the other side, the supply side, the greying of the population and the large number of baby boomers has resulted in thousands of highly experienced and competent people looking for an alternative to the city-based stressful corporate life. Many baby boomers have 20–30 years' experience in specialised areas. Some have been offered packages to facilitate their early retirement. They hunger for the possibility of living in the country or on the coast, in both Australia and New Zealand or in another country for some months of the year. They are ideally placed to enjoy their preferred lifestyle while as consultants they service clients in the major cities.

SOME TYPICAL CONSULTANT SITUATIONS

The six self-employed people described below are typical in as many ways as they are different. There are few generalisations one can make other than:

- most have at least ten years' experience at service delivery in their chosen field;
- they really enjoy service delivery;
- they have a degree of emotional autonomy. Their egos are such that they are happy to work by themselves without the accrued significance or sense of identity that comes from belonging to a big organisation.

ALAN, CONTRACT BOOKKEEPER
Alan worked with a major industrial company for twenty years, most of that time as an accountant in head office. During the 1990s he was assigned to project work involving financial management for teams laying cables for pay television and broadband internet access in major cities in Victoria and New South Wales. At the completion of this project he was physically exhausted and jumped at the offer of redundancy made as the company moved out of the cable-laying business. Alan has tertiary qualifications in accounting and business. With the introduction of GST at 1 July 2000, Alan decided to set up a bookkeeping business for micro businesses and SMEs.

Alan placed advertisements in the local newspapers and told his golfing friends he was going into business for himself. Within four months Alan ceased advertising and reset the parameters about what type of work he would accept. His life is full, but with more balance than it had during his days with the corporation. He plays golf on Wednesdays and Saturdays, and while he is very busy at the end of each quarter completing his clients' Business Activity Statements, he and his wife go away for regular short trips in their newly acquired recreation vehicle. Early in 2007, he moved from Melbourne to the country near Ballarat.

JUDY, MARKETING FREELANCER

Judy had an extensive career in marketing, becoming a senior account manager who would hold the clients' hands in managing their marketing projects from concept to completion. She withdrew from full-time business to focus more on her roles as homemaker and mother to three children. Now her children have reached adulthood, she and her husband spend some time travelling and pursuing other interests.

Judy has continued to work as a freelance marketer without the responsibility of full project management. She has maintained contact with her former colleagues, some of whom now have their own marketing businesses. They value her contribution in the nuts and bolts aspects of service delivery, freeing them up to do more of the relationship management aspects—holding their own clients' hands.

BILL, MANAGEMENT CONSULTANT

Bill has worked extensively in the agricultural sector as a manager of agribusinesses and as a consultant overseas for international agencies. After a somewhat nomadic life he decided that it would be good to work from one city in his own independent consultancy. Bill re-established contact with former clients, colleagues and acquaintances from his corporate life, and sent them business cards together with his profile document (see page 154). He also joined key organisations in his new city that gave him access to senior people in management and other consultants seeking to create business opportunities.

Much of Bill's previous work involved restructuring organisations and businesses in a distressed situation. His reading and research, combined with his corporate and consultative experience, resulted in the development of a series of workshops around the theme of Change Management. All these activities—the emailing, the networking and the seminars—have led to regular engagements with a variety of organisations around Australia. He stays in touch with his network by phone and by sending regular articles of interest, usually with a personal note attached.

ELLA, FREELANCE PROOFREADER

After teaching in Adelaide for fifteen years, Ella moved to Sydney and decided to undertake a career change. She enrolled in a short creative writing workshop where a chance meeting with someone who worked for a publishing company resulted in Ella doing proofreading for the publisher, which in turn led to obtaining similar work from other publishers. She has found that the work can be very demanding in terms of meeting deadlines, and she tries to avoid taking on too much. Ella loves the nature of the work as she is a great reader, likes the flexibility and variety which provide a strong contrast to her previous career, and is pleased not to have to deal with classroom stress.

JEFF, IT CONTRACTOR

During the 1990s, Jeff had extensive exposure to information systems development within a large financial institution. After working side-by-side for eighteen months with a number of IT contractors, he approached their employing organisation and was invited to join. It was pointed out that he could not be guaranteed more than the initial six-month contract which they were offering.

Market conditions boomed for computer consultants throughout the 1990s and although he was doing contracting work, Jeff was being rewarded with consultant rates of pay. He is in a much stronger financial position for having chosen contracting over his previous full-time employment. Interestingly, the financial institution he left was taken over by a company headquartered in a different city. Very few of his colleagues were offered positions under the new ownership as the IT work was totally absorbed by the new parent. In 2005 Jeff moved to London and is enjoying a contrasting lifestyle as well as an income in sterling that was in dollars in Australia.

ANNA, EVENTS CONSULTANT

After five years working in the hospitality industry as an assistant at a retreat resort, Anna completed an undergraduate course in recreation, physical education and hospitality management. In the first two years of her consultancy she worked as the relief manager at an inner-city hotel on the night-time roster. This part-time work ensured a regular minimum cash flow while she slowly built her consulting business. At the end of the two years she was able to drop the part-time work, having established a healthy client base with a wide assortment of clients. These included a 'meet at dinner' matchmaking service, an aged people's home, an adventure training company, a number of schools, a university, several travel agents and four large corporations. In performing her consultancy services, Anna designs, delivers and evaluates activities and events for many people and for many purposes.

DO YOU HAVE THE APPROPRIATE QUALITIES?

The following checklist is based on one originally developed by the US Small Business Administration. I have further developed it to apply to consultants where the main delivery relates to intellectual capital and the application of specialised knowledge, a further distinguishing feature of consultant businesses.

QUESTIONS
  1. Are you a self-starter?
     (a) I like to get things going. No one has to tell me.
     (b) Once we all get going, I put in as well as anyone else.
     (c) I'm easy going. I don't put myself out until I have to.

2. How organised are you?
   (a) I am a planner and generally approach all business matters methodically.
   (b) I work well with energy bursts and accomplish a lot quickly without the need for a formal plan.
   (c) I am a believer in 'what will be will be'. Most things turn out okay.
3. Are you a hard worker?
   (a) I can work when I have to. I am a 'smart worker'.
   (b) Yes.
   (c) Not really. Secretly I am a clock watcher and a solitaire player.
4. Are you decisive?
   (a) Yes.
   (b) Usually I am but it depends on what the decision is.
   (c) Can I have some more time to think about this?
5. How flexible are you?
   (a) I am used to fitting into different situations and then applying my skills.
   (b) Flexible within limits. Certain things need to be right for effective service delivery.
   (c) The idea that we can be all things to all people is false. I know how to do what I do and if I am given room I can get amazing things done.
6. Who is responsible for what you do?
   (a) As it is my business, I am.
   (b) I like to work in a cooperative and collaborative way. We share the decision-making, we share the work, we share the credit for success and we share the responsibility when things don't work out so well.
   (c) I am a one-person band. Often my work is so small relative to the operations of my very big corporate or government department clients that their priorities change. While I was once important to them, things move on and they no longer put their energy into my projects nor do they provide the resources previously agreed to and so I think they are probably more responsible for unsuccessful outcomes than I am.

7. How do you relate to other people?
   (a) Providing they are ethical, motivated and talented, I relate well.
   (b) There is something to like about all people and I usually find it.
   (c) I can get along with most people. If I meet someone particularly difficult in business I work within that situation as best I can and perhaps look for an earlier exit than originally envisaged.
8. Can you create enthusiasm about your work?
   (a) Yes. This work is enjoyable and rewarding for the client, stakeholders and for me. I find it easy to enthuse others because I am passionate about it.
   (b) Yes. The benefits are plain enough for anyone with some knowledge to see. I am against hard-sell tactics.
   (c) I am not into hype. Flashy American-inspired approaches have no place in Australia or New Zealand.
9. Do you follow through with all that you indicate?
   (a) Yes.
   (b) Mostly.
   (c) Yes, providing circumstances remain favourable.
10. Are you a risk taker?
   (a) I am prepared to take calculated risks and to manage the risks as best I can.
   (b) It is not about risk taking, it is about good planning.
   (c) I must admit I am a worrier and will usually rationalise the 'stay as we are' response to opportunities with significant risk.

COMMENTS

Q1:   Response (a) is more likely to lead to success with consulting. Response (b) can also work for someone seeking contracting opportunities but the first steps will have to come from you.

Q2:   The 'right answer' is (a) again, but many businesses can work with the (b) and (c) responses providing there is a lot of purposeful activity taking place. The rationale here is small business people are such a small yet flexible force within the economy that they may get many opportunities which see them fit perfectly into the plans of bigger entities which need the additional skills that small business people offer.

Q3:   Clearly (b) will be the formula correct answer, but (a) works as well.

Q4:   Those whose answer is (a) will use their time most effectively. In self-employment, it is only what one produces that earns the fees. All contracts will come to an end 'soon' and if there is the prospect of more work, only the effective and efficient workers will be offered a renewal.

Q5:   Response (a) is a good one for the contractor, while the consultant will normally answer (b). Response (c) sounds like someone who is not listening to the client situation; even if the statement were true, it is unlikely that the particular needs of the client would be met.

Q6:   Ultimately it is (a) so far as your consultant business is concerned. However, (b) may be a relevant response for the work you do with clients as distinct from the operation of your own business. Response (c) is both rational and plausible. However, it represents an attitude of passing off responsibility. It is *your* business, no one else's.

Q7:   Response (a) looks a little like the response of Narcissus—a famous self-admirer. Response (b) shows a positive attitude while (c), which is consistent with the goals of productive self-employment, may be the most realistic response for many experienced consultants.

Q8:   Response (a) is the most marketable, as it is often necessary to sell the idea to your client for adoption now. This usually involves showing them the benefits in their own words and in their own context. It might also involve some adjustment on your part to enable them to say yes now rather than to defer the decision. Response (b) is typical of someone technically proficient who has not taken time to understand the mind and the mood of the client, while response (c) fails to recognise that making the sale is part of the process of doing business. Every transaction involves a sale whereby the client says yes. In consultant businesses, this is often a benign process.

Q9:   Response (a) has to be adopted as the consultant's modus operandi. We need repeat business and we will be assessed on the basis of what we promise.

Q10: Responses here may differ according to the personality of the respondent. However, I like (a) because it recognises that there are risks and that they are outside our immediate area of influence. If (c) is the response you have chosen, and if you are a worrier, self-employment may not be a satisfactory option for you unless you choose to purchase an existing viable business that still has good prospects.

OVERHEARD IN THE VET'S WAITING ROOM:
'Tell me, now he's been neutered, does your old Tom still go out at night?'

'Oh yes. But now he's in the role of a consultant!'

Key points

- Being a consultant will see you positioned to obtain these benefits:
  - Choosing where you want to live
  - Doing the type of work you like
  - Choice of chasing the dollars or smelling the roses
  - Working productively
  - Having more control over your fate
  - The opportunity to choose your clients
  - Working at or near home
  - Variation in work, clients and places
  - Using little capital to start up your business
- To be successful you will need to have the desire to be self-employed, and have specialist skills and knowledge, good communication skills and persistence.
- If you choose a consultant career, always ask questions— ensure that you deliver what the client really needs, as opposed to what they say they need. Always test your assumptions.
- Consultant work is discontinuous and subject to change. There may be irregularity in your income, but you will have plenty of variety.
- Being a consultant costs much less than purchasing an existing business, but you will need access to funds to cover perhaps six to nine months of income as you establish your business.
- The market is strong for ancillary service providers, such as consultants and contractors, as larger businesses stay lean to focus on their core competencies.
- Answer the questionnaire to ascertain your suitability for self-employment.

2

ARE YOU READY FOR THIS?

You cannot change the direction of the wind. What you can do is trim your sails and change tack so that you can still be on target to your chosen destination.

Variation of an old adage

Those of you reading this book, whether you are a consultant already or an intending one, will most likely fall into one of six groups.

PASSIONATE PRACTITIONERS

You love your profession. It is your passion. You prefer doing it to being a manager. You are not so concerned about organisations; you are more concerned about the proper practice of your craft. You want to keep doing it, improvising, developing, improving standards, creating satisfaction whenever you deliver your service and enjoying the appreciation of the client. You also enjoy the feeling of a job well done.

LIFESTYLE SEEKERS

The idea of working for yourself excites you. You want change, change that mainly involves freedom from the conventions of normal work. You want to do the job without being involved in politics. You are happy to work flat out some of the time and you would like to go slower at other times. You want balance, to do other things in your life, to get off the treadmill. Or, you want to raise your children—hands-on! At the least, you are having thoughts along these lines.

RESTRUCTURED RECRUITS

Employment conditions in your industry have changed radically. In short, if you wish to continue doing what you have done in your career, you need to become a self-employed contractor. This is a turning point in your career and it offers you the opportunity to build your own business, be it small or large. It also offers you the opportunity to become a member of one of the two groups above.

RELUCTANT RECRUITS

Things have not gone well for you recently. You are no longer employed, having been an employee all your working life. You also notice that everyone you have met on your job search is younger than you, including the members of interview panels. Self-employment is looming as the only realistic option for getting back to work in the short to medium term.

BUSINESS-BUILDING ENTREPRENEURS

What you want to do now is to build a business. You seek the control over your life that the lifestyle seeker wants. You have the passion for a job done well that the passionate practitioner exudes. You have the opportunities before you of which the restructured recruit is aware. You share the view that the only way forward for you is this option. It is an opportunity to create an asset that will have considerable value in five years' time. This idea excites you!

NOT FOR ME, THANK YOU!

Someone gave you this book. They thought you might have been interested, but you are not. In this case, would you please wipe the cover and think about who you can pass it on to. Think of someone you know who hungers for a better working life and may or may not have realised that they need a change.

For most of you, your area of specialisation is set. It is advisable, however, not to confine yourself to a single activity but to develop your business into two or three areas of specialisation. This means that if one area goes slow you will not be stranded, as you have other services you can perform. You can read further about specialisation later in this chapter.

Reluctant recruits are often very successful in making the transition to self-employment. Facing the alternative of premature retirement, unemployment benefits and a feeling of failure, they can become as motivated and persistent as any business builder.

Lifestyle seekers, however, may be in a quandary about what to do. You may not see much evidence of people with your skills working successfully for themselves. It is also possible that you have generalised your thinking about your career to date. The story about Brendan illustrates how the label given to a particular career may obscure the range of skills developed by a practitioner.

LIFE AFTER THE ARMY

Brendan had been an infantryman for fifteen years, and had always regarded his training as preparing him for soldiering. But there was more to army training than that, he discovered.

As part of the training for his resettlement into civilian life, Brendan had to make a list of all the jobs he had held during his army career, then identify the skills he had used to perform each job. Like the other members of the defence forces, he essentially undertook a new job every three years. In each job he learned new skills.

Brendan had spent considerable time in the army as a trainer, as a manager and as a project manager. His positions usually required a high degree of organisational skill and it was identified that he had considerable experience and competence in the field of logistics. In his time on active duty as a peacekeeper in the Middle East, Brendan had also led teams in the clearing of land mines. This was a task that required great concentration, a methodical approach and attention to detail.

As he moved into the civilian job market Brendan was offered a job with the Electoral Commission, and one in security.

However, he and two colleagues set up a security business, gaining contracts at the Sydney Olympic and Melbourne Commonwealth Games. They are now security advisers to events managers.

Lifestyle seekers and reluctant recruits can go one of two ways. You can either continue to perform in your area or opt to do something totally new. Continuing to practise in a familiar field will see you make a reasonably smooth transition to consulting. If you like the idea of making a switch, however, one of the first things I suggest you do is sit down with a group of friends and see how many people you can list who have made career changes. Professional sports people do it too as their performance tapers off. I suppose 90 per cent of politicians do this when they enter politics. (You can decide whether they have done so successfully!)

At the everyday level, I know two members of the police force who bought management rights to a block of holiday units on Queensland's Gold Coast. I met a former music teacher and her restaurateur husband who use their people, management and creative skills to run a caravan park in the Snowy Mountains. Another who comes to mind is a former trade commissioner who gives advice to olive growers in the south-west of Western Australia. She is also a judge in olive-tasting competitions and shows.

Each of these people is doing something different in their second career. The ex-police husband and wife find managing their units on the Gold Coast a demanding job, but see that they have accelerated their retirement; they will be able to afford it twenty years earlier than if they had remained in the police force. They admit that their expectations have also changed, and may continue as unit managers for longer than they originally thought in order to amass more capital, and will perhaps scale down rather than retire. Their excellent interpersonal skills, their ability to handle groups of people, to organise cleaners, tenants and landlords, and to comply with myriad government regulations suit them for this business.

The olive consultant is passionate about her work in a field completely new to her when she started. Her extensive knowledge is the result of dedicated learning over the five years since she left her career as a trade commissioner. Her professionalism is very evident, and she has demonstrated her commitment by establishing her own olive grove and a showroom for the sale of olive-related products.

WHAT WOULD YOU LIKE TO DO?

Now is one of those rare times in your life when you have the freedom to set off in a new direction—to do something totally different. It may be something that you have always wanted to do.

To take that step and do what you always wanted to do will involve considerable risks. The biggest of these risks is that if you pursue a different course you will effectively be out of the market if you ever wish to return to your traditional professional area. Short breaks are possible to overcome, but after a protracted period you will lose touch with the cutting edge and lose your contacts; favoured clients will have formed relationships with your competitors.

A related risk is that you may have no network support in your new field. You may also be offered substitutes inferior to your true goal, and you could be lured away from where you really want to go.

Notwithstanding the risks, the opportunity is here. It will be made easier if your dependants are self-funding, your mortgage is low or paid off and you have some savings that you can access should business be slow.

If this is something you have always wanted to do, then you will, by definition, know what it is. To receive some inspiration in this area, it may be well worthwhile going for a one-month holiday. A friend of mine often says:

In the first week of the holiday, all the stress drops off.
The second week is when you start to enjoy yourself.
In the third week, you contemplate why you are living the life you lead.
And the final week is when you decide to make big changes in your life.

Over to you. Take a holiday.

ARE YOU READY FOR A CHANGE IN YOUR LIFE?

There is a commonly accepted index of stress which rates a major career change as one of the highest causes of stress. With or without the mid-life crisis, you have a recipe for a person not clear about what to do with their lives. Are *you* prepared for such a major change in your life?

The diagram of the change model can be applied to those of you in the third and fourth groups, and indeed to anybody currently experiencing changes. Its origins lie in the grief model work of Elisabeth Kubler Ross, and were further developed by Scott and Jaffe.[1]

The model suggests that someone experiencing change will pass through four distinct phases. There is some debate about whether the progression is as linear as it appears in this diagram; different people will also spend longer in some quadrants than in others. It is also possible to slip back along the curve to a previous quadrant.

The first quadrant is known as *Denial*. At this point the individual experiencing change is shocked, expresses disbelief, and will carry on as normal. There may be some withdrawal and there is rarely any moving forward.

Change model

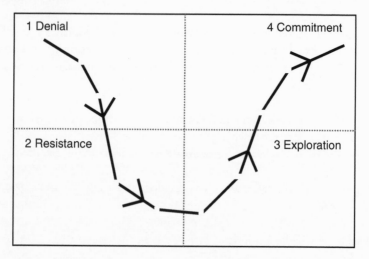

A situation demonstrating the shock reaction occurred early in the downsizing phase in the finance sector. Employees were assembled in the theatre of their company building, told they had been dismissed and then ushered into a large room where psychologists and counsellors waited to interview them. Clearly collectively shocked, the now ex-employees shunned the counsellors and headed out of the building in hurt and angry groups. The process was inappropriate, worsening the situation. Its only redeeming aspect was that it forced human resources practitioners to examine their methodologies for dismissing people.

In the second quadrant, called *Resistance*, the individual loses focus, becomes resentful and typically apportions blame to all others in their life. There is anger, anxiety and lethargy. The reason for the lack of energy is that nothing is seen to matter any more. It is suggested that sabotage may be part of this picture. You may have heard of people being taken straight out the door, not allowed to go back to their desks. This is apparently done to avoid sabotage of the company's information systems by an aggrieved former worker. A tad insensitive, however.

The change may be of a medical nature—a victim of a heart attack or a stroke will also pass through these phases. I remember my father threatening to walk under a bus as he recovered slowly from a stroke, behaviour cited as an example of the sabotage reaction. This is a man who had survived cruelty and deprivation as a prisoner of war in Changi, the Burma Railroad and the coal mines in Japan.

When people experiencing change are in these first two quadrants, they are concerned with what has happened to them. Their casual talk is of their former workplace, about how 'those people back there wouldn't know what they were doing' and how the whole place is going to fall apart. It is very difficult for someone in that position to contemplate looking forwards. If this has happened to you, it is unlikely that you will pick up this book until you move into quadrant three.

The right-hand side of the diagram reflects the person starting to look to the future and starting to talk about their plans. Quadrant three, called *Exploration*, is characterised by bursts of energy, false starts, over-preparation and perhaps too many things going on—a lack of clarity. The future now has a series of moving parameters and is a little blurry, but in contrast to their position on the left-hand side of the diagram the person sees that there actually is a future.

Finally the person moves into the top right-hand quadrant where there is *Commitment* to a goal, a purpose. There is focus and order and the horizon extends out for years instead of the much shorter horizon in quadrant three.

The value of this model is that it explains to anyone who is experiencing change why they have so many different attitudes over the period following change. It is of little value to be told to 'snap out of it' and to 'stop feeling sorry for yourself' if you are on the left-hand side of the diagram. Sometimes people go straight from quadrant one to quadrant four: often men following a relationship break-up. Psychologists say that if this happens, the resistance and the exploration will probably come later. It is more common for women to go through the four quadrants, they say.

It is normal to be blurry. It is okay. Let the exploration process work itself out. Through contemplating many differing scenarios and developing some of them, you will ultimately come to a new future about which you can be confidently optimistic.

WHERE HAVE YOU BEEN AND WHAT DID YOU DO THERE?

Having identified what you are doing here, and how you feel about it, let's look at your track record and where you have come from. For most consultants, the way forward is an extension of the past. You continue to do as a self-employed person what you used to do as an employee. You know how to do it, you know the industry and, most importantly, you are known in the industry.

To start this process, you should now prepare a breakdown of your skills. Use five columns to list your jobs and the industry in which you worked at the time; the nature of the tasks performed; the skills you used in doing those tasks; what your achievements were; and where else you could do these things. This will effectively be a list of your skill sets and of the outcomes you can produce, or contribute significantly towards producing. The table on pages 30–1 gives three examples.

On the basis that you will be more successful at the things you like doing and that you do well, highlight the tasks that you enjoyed doing and the ones that you were good at. You now have a list that shows your areas of specialisation. Having an industry specialisation and activity and skills specialisations gives you credibility in the eyes of potential hirers. You can also have the basis of your three to five page capability statement or profile document as described in Chapter 7.

In the example on pages 30–1, the three people have activity specialisations in property maintenance, canteen management and financial administration respectively. Their industry specialisations are local government, education and health but their skills have application beyond those immediate industries. It is possible to do this with most individuals and, arguably, with all people, even if they have not been in the work force, although some claims will be more convincing than others.

Clients want skilled people who have done the things the client needs done before. It is up to the individual to show how their skill set has application beyond the immediate area in which it was acquired.

HOW DO I SHOW MY EXPERIENCE IS RELEVANT?

People conducting interviews for any position want to find out what the candidate can do and how that relates to the job in question. This applies to those seeking consultancy engagements just as much as to the permanent job seeker.

One of the standard interview techniques is known as the STAR tactic for personnel selection. The questions are asked in a sequence so that the interviewee will reveal what their achievements are and the context in which they were made. The acronym stands for:

S   **Situation** in which the interviewee worked
T   **Task** the interviewee performed
A   **Action** the interviewee took
R   **Results** that were achieved (by the interviewee)

Example of skills identification

Place, position & industry	Task	Skills	Achievements	Transferable to
Southern City Council, Property Manager, Local Government	Property maintenance management: meeting performance objectives related to service, time, money and quality.	• Contract preparation • Task description • Negotiating commercial contracts • Management of contract teams • Evaluating standards of work	• Improved maintenance as assessed • Reduced overall expenditure • Increased productivity • Reduced lost time • Did so over 4 years	• All businesses using outsourced providers • Both gov't & private industry • Funds management • Investment management • Real estate/ property • Hospitality/ tourism • Aged care • Construction
Inner South Secondary College, Canteen Manager, School Canteen Supervisor	Manage the school canteen by offering healthy cuisine that is well patronised by the school population, on a breakeven plus 3% basis.	• Menu selection • Food ordering and preparation • Working with volunteers • Selection of and liaison with volunteers	• Re-appointed 5 times for 5 years • Increased sales • Increased number of patrons • Developed recess trade	• Canteens: schools, corporations • Restaurants, cafeterias, cafes, sandwich shops, milk bars, catering, institutions

		• Collection, reporting and banking of moneys	• Managed GST provisions	• Volunteer organisations
			• Offered management positions in other canteens	
Royal City Central Hospital, Financial Accountant, Health	Financial reporting and budget control.	• Collection & interpretation of data	• Brought budget under control	• All businesses (which measure performance financially)
		• Recording of information	• Met objectives as required	• Health-related, including medical practices, hospitals, health funds, aged care institutions
		• Monitoring expenditure and revenue	• Increased efficiency	• Bureaucracies
		• Account collections	• Trained personnel to record financial transactions	• Gov't bureaucracies inc. education, local government (one for each minister at each level of government)
		• Reporting to CFO	• Managed GST provisions when introduced	• Recently corporatised entities
		• Explaining finance aspects to own department	• Reduced waste	
			• Reduced graft!	

You can use the STAR tactic yourself, applying it to your list of previous jobs to complete *vignettes*—mini case studies or short summaries of your achievements. Preparation of such vignettes is a continuous task for any consultant or job seeker. (People in permanent employment will also benefit from their frequent preparation for use either in performance appraisals or their next career move.) By preparing these vignettes you will be ready for the questions from the interviewers. Putting them in writing gives you an excellent marketing tool that will help your prospective client or hirers see what you can do for them.

The two completed vignettes presented below will make it easier to do your own.

LIBRARIAN VIGNETTE

Situation Assistant Librarian in the Research and Development section of a major corporation, in charge of Special Projects.

Task The company acquired a coal mine in Indonesia. My job was to source information that would enable our people to work more effectively when they arrived in Indonesia.

Action By using the Internet and other sources I found information relevant to expats living in Indonesia, and the services to assist them, both prior to departure and upon arrival. It included all matters relating to where they would live: education, health, recreation, customs, expectations, language training, employment and all related issues for the families and partners who accompanied our people. I arranged for briefing sessions, and an orientation program for all concerned. I then designed and produced an interactive DVD for those unable to attend the program and to allow for consolidation and further exploration of the issues at home and in their own time.

Results The company asked me to produce a similar program for all seven of our offshore locations. We also had the relevant government department visit to see how it was done. I have testimonials from the Head Librarian and from the HR director acknowledging my work.

FREELANCE DESIGNER VIGNETTE

Situation My job was as architect and designer for fit-outs of new houses on housing estates for a major developer of housing projects.

Task To offer a customised service to prospective home purchasers both within and outside our developments. The company had sold fifteen houses within one development to members of an ethnic minority group that had special needs.

Action I interviewed each of the families that had purchased a house and determined their requirements. I then prepared draft designs, checked them with the clients and then went to the local authority to seek approval. At first it was denied. Then, with my boss's approval, I prepared a special presentation for the city councillors, informing them of the issue and of the new 'non-conforming' plans.

Results Approval was granted and the transaction with the ethnic community was mirrored in another capital city. The company asked me to develop the presentation concept and it was used in all future meetings with the local government authorities in the areas where we created residential developments.

Compilation of a number of these vignettes is excellent preparation both for deciding what you want to do and for marketing yourself, either in writing or in person. Another organisation uses a similar methodology which they call PAR (Problem, Action, Result). Vignettes are a very effective tool for conveying user-friendly information about the competencies of people in the workforce. If you are choosing to work as a consultant, you can still use your previous employment history as the source of your vignettes, as they describe what *you* can do as distinct from what the organisation did. As it should be easy for the reader or interviewer to see the relevance of the vignette to their need, you will need a number of them and be selective in their use.

You now have your first marketing tools. You can also see from them that there is a career for you as a consultant, in the sense that there are discrete projects that you could do for clients.

It is important to prepare marketing documents other than the résumé or CV. Hirers of consultants are looking for someone to solve a problem or to meet a short-term need. They can usually see both the start and the end of the project. They are focused on the project and not beyond that. Therefore the best marketing tools for you to use are those that are focused on that service provision. These will be your vignettes and your capability statement or profile document, which are about what can be done rather than where you were five years ago. The CV or résumé is really the tool of the permanent job seeker and I recommend you don't use it unless it is specified as a requirement.

IF I TAKE THIS STEP, WHAT SORT OF CONSULTANT WILL I BE?

Will I be a consultant, a freelancer or a contractor? Am I a high profiler or a low profiler?

In Chapter 1 a distinction was made between the three types of professional service provision. To re-cap, the consultant sets the parameters, the contractor works within them. The consultant solves the problem, the contractor implements the solution. You sometimes perform both roles. The freelancer can be at either end of this spectrum and is more likely to be in a field related to the arts or in the communications industry.

Consultants tend to be high profilers. That is, they compete on their reputations and build profile and identity in their market segments. Contractors tend to be lower profile. Freelancers vary from being highly differentiated and well known to being part-time casual-rate workers. That is, they can be either high or low profilers. High profilers tend to have shorter engagements and be paid more per day. Low profilers tend to have longer engagements and be paid less. Their full-year incomes will reflect how many days they are engaged.

AM I A PROBLEM SOLVER OR AN IMPLEMENTER OF SOLUTIONS?

The following diagram shows the relationship between the four roles that consultants (or freelancers) perform.[2] For ease of understanding, you might like to write the word 'What' on the horizontal axis—that is, as we move to the right, the client has a clearer idea about what they want. Similarly, on the vertical axis write 'How'. As we move up, the client has a clearer idea about how the consultancy should be undertaken—the process to be followed.

The four roles of the consultant

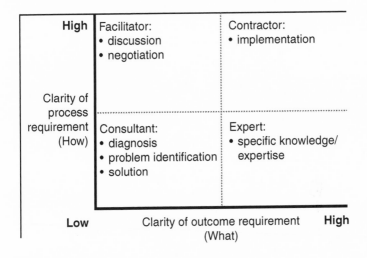

The bottom left-hand quadrant, where the outcome required by the client is relatively unclear and the means or processes by which the outcome will be achieved are also unclear, illustrates a consultant's role. The consultant will conduct research to gather data in order to diagnose what the problem or solution might be. Once that has been recognised and client commitment achieved, then the project is free to proceed with implementation through to completion and subsequent evaluation.

In the top right-hand quadrant, where the outcome required is very clear, as is the means to achieve it, the client's need is for someone to perform the role of contractor. In such an instance, it is highly likely that the quality of work which the contractor is to deliver, and the time in which it is to be delivered, are predetermined. This leaves price as the only variable aspect.

The other two quadrants depict the roles that consultants perform in the course of service delivery. When the client is very clear about their preferred outcome but does not know how the consultant achieves that result, the consultant performs the role of expert. In such a role the consultant is highly regarded, subject to a satisfactory result being obtained. If there is an error, then the consultant must take full blame as there is not the shared ownership that results from working closely with the client in the roles of pure consultant or facilitator.

In the top left quadrant, the consultant facilitates meetings with stakeholders and the client in order to solve the problem and clarify directions. Client ownership of the consultant work is high when this method of service delivery is used, but it can be slow and there is no guarantee that a workable solution will be found. It is best viewed as one of the tools consultants can use to achieve the desired results for the client.

WHAT ARE THE REQUIRED SKILLS?

All consultants require four major skill bases.

1. PROFESSIONAL COMPETENCE

This first one is their special skill base and is known as the area of professional or technical competence. The skill has been acquired by the consultant practising a certain type of activity, training in the activity, and discussing and thinking about the activity. The key factor is experience. Most consultants have in excess of seven years' experience in their particular field. It is rare for high profile consultants to be younger than 30 years of age.

Younger consultants normally fall into two categories. The first group are often highly qualified and very bright employees of the major international consulting firms. They generally receive their directions from the principals in their organisation and their time is spent mainly in the implementation phase of consulting. The second category comprises gifted, bright and innovative computer or other design specialists who are likely to be functioning at all phases of the process.

In my experience, high profiler consultants who say they are generalists rather than specialists turn out, upon further probing, to actually be specialists. They are often specialists in human resources, organisational development, business processes, management or project managers.

Each HR practitioner usually has a range of HRD (human resources development) or HRM (human resources management) skills. The range of skills is usually so broad that the person appears to be a generalist. When that person is seen as one provider within a large organisation it is more apparent that they are an HR specialist. Management consultants, OD specialists and business systems or process specialists all can claim to be generalist yet have quite specialist skills in their broad areas.

Similarly, project managers have a specialist skills set involving knowledge of how to successfully manage a project on time, within budget and in accordance with the specifications. Competent project managers can apply the skills in a wide range of areas. Many senior defence force personnel make excellent project managers in business and community organisations.

2. INTERPERSONAL SKILLS

These enable you to develop a relationship with the client so that you will gain their confidence sufficiently to be engaged, and so that the project can be successfully implemented. Clearly, a major interpersonal skill is effective communication skills. This is made up of the ability to listen and understand what the client is saying so that you can clearly understand the client's needs, aspirations and context, and the ability to communicate your own message effectively through a combination of verbal and body language. Ideally you can relate to the client in such a way that mutual trust is developed between the two of you.

Other necessary interpersonal skills are the ability to manage a group of people, to successfully resolve conflict, to negotiate with stakeholders and to achieve a measure of influence.

3. BUSINESS SKILLS

Strategy, marketing, pricing and management—which is what most of this book is about.

4. CONSULTING SKILLS

You will also need consulting skills. This is the ability to complete the stages of the consulting process so that you maximise the probability of success in your work. These skills are described in Chapter 10.

DO I PRESENT AS A SPECIALIST OR AS A GENERALIST?

The answer to this question will be related to whether you take the higher profile or lower profile route. The higher profile consultant will need to have definition, to give a very clear message about what they can do. Lower profile consultants are really offering themselves as an additional pair of hands and will therefore wish to convey that they have a wide range of skills and can apply themselves to many tasks in the industry or work situation.

ADVANTAGES OF POSITIONING AS A SPECIALIST

1. It helps build your profile (what the market knows about you). The market has a clear identification of what you do and who you are professionally.
2. As you specialise you gain more knowledge, acquire more skill and become more expert. To this extent, specialisation will become a self-fulfilling prophecy.
3. You are perceived as being more expert and therefore as more useful to clients.
4. Your professional development is more focused, covering fewer areas and perhaps costing less.
5. Prospective clients will want you on their networks, whereas the generalist will be regarded as being just like them, nothing particularly special.
6. You can charge a premium for specialised service delivery.
7. Your operation is more efficient because you develop standard methodologies and products. It is also probable that you can be more effective and efficient in the diagnostic stage.
8. It is easier to market because your target market can see how you can assist, your market is more clearly defined and it may be smaller.
9. As the market is smaller, you will need to travel to lots of places. This is considered an advantage at this early stage!

DISADVANTAGES OF POSITIONING
AS A SPECIALIST

1. There is a greater risk of obsolescence. This can be either technical obsolescence, where new technology renders your skills obsolete, or due to a market shift where the trend moves away from your skills even though they can still deliver the promised outcomes. CAD (computer-aided design) technology has rendered many designers obsolete. Latin teachers have less work than previously as students favour business and IT subjects.
2. You may be perceived as lacking strategic vision and seen to have only one solution. The trainer will continue to run training workshops when the real problem may be a combination of issues relating to personnel, systems and flawed strategy.
3. In like manner, the market may typecast you as being over-specialised and not capable of doing those other things at which you are proficient. You may be overlooked for many jobs.
4. As the market is smaller for a specialist, there are fewer opportunities.
5. One less-than-favourable outcome and you are finished (because the niche is so small).
6. Burn-out and boredom may occur as you engage in highly repetitive work.
7. Too much travel!

AND THE RECOMMENDATION IS . . .?

As a high profiler, position yourself as a specialist, but have two or three areas of specialisation in case one area goes quiet. You can specialise in a number of activities or in a number of industries or some combination thereof. For example, you may be a trainer specialising in business skills training. The specialisation is an activity within which there are a number of sub-specialisations. These could be training in communication, leadership and management skills. These may be offered across a wide range of industries, which means you are not limited by industry or regional specialisation.

Specialisation might be an activity (what you do); an industry in which you do it; and/or a region where you work.

For lower profile contractors, take a more generalist route but have specialist skills. Clients will want specific specialist skills. It is also useful for contractors to be able to refer to one or more industry specialisations when discussing the prospect of engagement with a client. The contractor who knows the industry context, the jargon, the pricing, the industrial relations and other political issues will arguably settle in sooner and make meaningful contributions more quickly.

At the earlier stages of your business, your outlook will be rather blurry. This is because you are not yet sure of what to promote and what clients will want. As time passes and you receive engagements you can speak about what you have done with considerable confidence.

Key points

- Identify where you are in your career. Are you a passionate practitioner, lifestyle seeker, restructured recruit, reluctant recruit or a business-building entrepreneur?
- Consider what is involved emotionally and intellectually in changing direction in your career and therefore in your life.
- You have marketable skills. Decide what they are; write up mini case studies of how you applied your skills (vignettes).
- Look at your skills, consider your preferences and determine where you would actually prefer to work.
- Decide on whether you want to accept the responsibility, pressure and rewards of being a high-profile consultant or freelancer, or whether you would be happier with less pressure and lower rewards, but only a little less responsibility, as a low-profile contractor or freelancer.
- Consider what areas of activity you would specialise in. Try to find three, but realise at this early stage that it is normal to be blurred in your focus.

BUSINESS PLAN

If you don't design your own life plan, chances are you'll fall into someone else's plan. And guess what they may have planned for you? Not much!

Jim Rohn[1]

The plan is useless; it's the planning that's important.

Dwight D. Eisenhower[2]

WHAT IS THE BUSINESS PLAN?

A business plan is the summary document about what you will do in business. It will include the answers to the questions posed by Rudyard Kipling's 'six honest serving-men . . . What and Why and When and How and Where and Who'.[3] Add to that, 'How Often'.

- What you will do: what you will offer?
- Why will you do this: your purposes in being in business?
- When will the business commence, what hours will you keep?
- How will you operate the business: will you have other staff?
- Where will you operate from and where will you provide your services?

- Who will be your customers? Who will produce the goods and services?
- Who will do what in the business?
- How often will you review the progress and direction of your business?

Darwinian thinking tells us that it is the most adaptive that will survive—not the strongest, not the wealthiest, not the most intelligent. As with many things in life, in business there is a strong link between your strengths and your weaknesses. While as an independent you have a weakness in scale, which is the lack of capacity to take on big projects, you are more likely to have the flexibility that comes with being small and unencumbered. It takes little to change the direction of your business and this is a big plus. Your business plan should be there to give you direction, but to survive you must adapt to the market. Adaptability and an attitude that accepts change will be key success factors—issues that are critical to your success.

These factors lead me to the view that a brief plan is a better plan. Detailed plans get lost in their own detail. For years my business plan has been a four-page document that is constantly reviewed and modified. The Mindshop organisation has a one-page business plan template which is essentially the three-part gap-analysis model: Where do you want to be (say in three years)? Where are you now? What is the gap and what steps need to be taken to bridge the gap? This is your one- (to four- or five-) page plan!

The business plan is a product of the planning process discussed in the next section. Undertake this first and then you can produce your written plan. It will have a full version which you can modify to take to your banker should you need to apply for some form of financial accommodation, and a shorter version that you work with day to day.

FIRST, YOU UNDERTAKE THE PLANNING PROCESS

You have probably done this in your old job—stifling the odd yawn. Well, this time it's for real and very worthwhile. Much of the process you will have already done intuitively as you contemplate how you can make your consultancy work. Here are the steps you take to prepare your plan:

Strategic planning
1. Develop vision
2. Confirm values
3. Define mission statement—purpose
4. Set goals
5. Environmental scan: external and internal
6. Identify key success factors
7. Review goals
8. Develop and determine strategies
9. Create action plans—set targets
10. Implement
Continuously review

Planning is a continuous process. Here is what you can do at each stage and the reason, as a consultant, why you should!

1. DEVELOP AND DEFINE YOUR VISION

Vision is big-picture activity—broad in scope and lacking in detail. It often consists of a number of very broad goals and may include references to the following issues:

- Creation of a viable form of self-employment.
- Doing work that interests and perhaps excites you: in short, pursuing your passion.
- Working in fields in which you excel, or have considerable talent.
- Achieving leadership status or some form of recognition in the community (this may be the community in which you live, your family or your profession).
- Making a lot of money, creating an ideal lifestyle, or whatever you consider worthwhile striving to achieve.

The vision is what you are creating. It will remain constant and so will your values. Everything after that in this hierarchy of planning events is subject to change, however.

2. CONFIRM YOUR VALUES AND STANDARDS

This is a list of the values that you hold in conducting your business. Professional service guru David Maister defines a value as a non-negotiable minimum standard to which all your work and dealings must apply. Maister says that a value is not a high aspiration you plan to strive for: that is a dream and may be referred to in the vision section.[4]

Values may relate to levels of technical competence or to how dealings with clients are conducted, both on a business basis and on a personal basis. Some examples are:

- To produce work at the highest standard.
- To avoid conflicts of interest by having an interval of at least six months when working for competing clients. (This may arise relatively often because you tend to develop areas of specialisation in both the activities you perform and the industries in which you offer them.)
- A complete set of performance standards, relating to how the telephone is answered, mail responded to, handling of queries, contents of offers to clients and billing procedures.
- If clients are not totally happy, then ask them to pay what they think the work is worth. (*Note:* Often the work of the small independent is rescheduled or redirected. This may be because the focus of the corporation has changed since you were engaged and you are merely a drop of water in their ocean of activity. Be careful therefore about making such promises.)

I have written down values I consider important. One is treating others as I would like to be treated. Practically, values help make the decision to join others as clients or joint venturers. Differences of opinion in projects are often related to different views about what is important in life. Having an awareness of values can prevent many of the dilemmas that can arise in business situations.

3. DEFINE YOUR PURPOSE OR MISSION STATEMENT

The best way to describe this is to call it your purpose statement—what you are doing, how and for whom. It is just one or two sentences and functions as a reminder, to help you get back on track and solve issues that arise in the day-to-day conduct of your business.

While the Vision and Values are 'about you', the Mission is about your services and clients. An example of the mission or purpose statement for an independent service provider might be: 'To provide a full range of bookkeeping services to small businesses in the Gold Coast region'. This helps the focus in the sense that if one of the bookkeeper's clients offered work for one day a week, entering data into their company database, the bookkeeper could instantly see that this was not in the original plan for the business and thus would not take on that type of work while there was the opportunity to seek out more clients requiring full bookkeeping services.

Some mission statements include references to 'quality' or to being 'the best' in the region. It is fine if you wish to do that. My own view is that it should be assumed that the service provider will always act with integrity, honesty and in the best interests of the client, produce quality work, and be continually improving.

Vision is big picture and about where you are headed in three to five years. The mission is about what you will do now to implement the vision. Goals are the detail of the vision and mission.

4. SET GOALS TO GIVE FOCUS

The goals of your business will be related to the achievement of the vision. Goals are the outcomes you want to achieve in the next period, be it one year or three. A good way to make goals is for them to be SMART (that is, Specific, Measurable, Achievable, Realistic, and Time defined).

Some examples of goals relevant to you might be:

Goal 1 To achieve an income level of $90 000 per annum by the end of my third year in business. (Many of you will need or want more, others may aim for less.)

Goal 2 To be engaged by three clients for more than ten days each in the second half of this financial year. (Such a goal will see you on your way to viability as you gain the requisite number of days; if your daily rate is realistic, then your other plans relating to cash flow and profitability will be likely to succeed.)

Goal 3 To have a total number of days of engagement in my first year of 60, in my second year 100 days, and in my third year 130 days.

Goal 4 To offer services under the banner of two professional associations (or other major industry participants) within the next six months.

Goal 5 To work at my business on not more than four days per week on average so that I do not work in the business for more than 176 days in the next twelve months; I will use that extra day to (insert favoured non-work activity that can be conducted on a one-day-per-week basis).

5. UNDERTAKE AN ENVIRONMENTAL SCAN

This is your market research. It will include research of the marketplace, including client needs, market size, competition, current pricing levels, potential gaps, and the possibilities for alliances and leverage (environmental analysis). It will also include an analysis of your own capacity and situation.

A popular way to format your personal analysis is through a process called the SWOT analysis, whereby you identify your Strengths, Weaknesses, Opportunities and Threats. (The SWOT is part of your day-to-day plan, not the plan your banker sees.)

On page 48 is a sample SWOT conducted for a consultant. Yours will be similar in part. Have someone who knows you help you do it; this should make the result more objective and therefore more valuable.

SWOT analysis

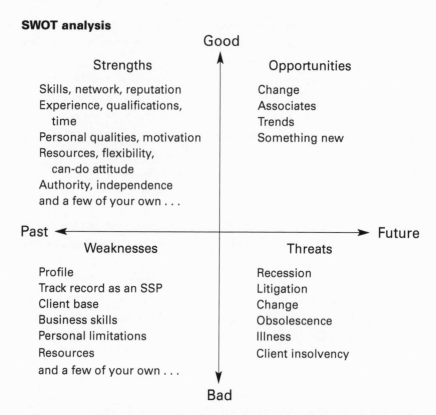

Good

Strengths

Skills, network, reputation
Experience, qualifications,
    time
Personal qualities, motivation
Resources, flexibility,
    can-do attitude
Authority, independence
and a few of your own . . .

Opportunities

Change
Associates
Trends
Something new

Past ◄─────────────────────────► Future

Weaknesses

Profile
Track record as an SSP
Client base
Business skills
Personal limitations
Resources
and a few of your own . . .

Threats

Recession
Litigation
Change
Obsolescence
Illness
Client insolvency

Bad

After you have completed the analysis process, the information can be used to help you capitalise on your strengths, overcome your weaknesses, develop your opportunities and manage threats. Threats need to be identified, as does the probability of their occurring and their likely impact. This allows you to plan what to do in the event that they do occur. It is not good enough to simply try to avoid them.

There is a famous case of managing threat involving the Royal Dutch Shell Company. In 1973, OPEC (the Organization of Petroleum Exporting Countries) decided to increase the price of crude oil threefold virtually overnight. World economies were thrown into chaos, and so were the oil companies. Except for Shell, that is, because they had drawn up a plan to deal with such an event. They had conducted 'scenario planning' a few years earlier, and one of the scenarios planned for the unlikely event of the oil price increasing significantly overnight. Shell emerged from the crisis as the leading oil company.

One of the threats you will face is the loss of a major client. Many factors can cause such a loss: takeover, resignation, promotion or transfer of your key contact, downfall in their sales or funding, a change of direction of their business or simply a desire on their part to do things differently.

By completing the threats part of the SWOT analysis, you will hopefully face far fewer surprises in your business.

6. IDENTIFY KEY SUCCESS FACTORS (KSFs), THE THINGS YOU MUST GET RIGHT

These are the aspects of the business which must be attained for it to be successful. KSFs are also know as KRAs: key result areas. If your business is cleaning swimming pools, you need to understand pool chemicals, you need to be at the client's address on the agreed date and the pools need to be clean. For most service providers the main KSF will be delivering what you promise.

A typical KSF for you as an independent service provider is the need for leverage through some other entities. There are many markets in your target area and it is costly to communicate with them. An effective and inexpensive way to do this is by leverage through organisations and businesses that also communicate with that market. For example, a personal computer specialist who assembles and modifies hardware, installs software and gives advice on program operation and customisation could leverage through suppliers of computer equipment.

Other KSFs include a client contact program. If you stay in touch with your clients they will be more likely to make referrals and to call you when they have another need for the service you provide. It is advisable to have ongoing marketing activities as there will always be some attrition of your client base; you will want to obtain new clients from the perspectives of both self-development and maintaining your own level of interest.

It is also important to ensure that your client base is sufficiently large to avoid earning more than 80 per cent of your income from one client group. In such a case it is probable that the Tax Office would not regard you as being a legitimate business and would treat you as an employee for tax purposes. This means that many expenditure items are disallowed as a write-off against income.

Similarly, your client base should be varied so that you can avoid being over-dependent on one or two clients. This will enable you to manage the risk of them ceasing to engage you for whatever reason.

7. REVIEW YOUR GOALS IN THE LIGHT OF ALL THIS PLANNING!

Reviewing your goals becomes a reality check in light of what you have discovered about the marketplace and about yourself. It may be that the four-day week will have to wait until the second year of your business, or that the dollars you plan to make need to be adjusted down. You may also come to an awareness that you need to form an alliance, undertake some form of self-education or acquire extra equipment that will enable you to offer a complete range of services within your chosen area.

For example, a prospective bookkeeper might need additional competency in, say, QuickBooks, having already mastered MYOB and Microsoft Money. The contractor who can maintain diesel and petrol generators may need to form a partnership with an engineer who can service electric generators. The specialist in the performing arts may need to form an association with some jazz musicians to satisfy a client who wants a change from the chamber music ensemble they regularly engage.

8. DEVELOP STRATEGIES SO THAT YOU CAN ACHIEVE YOUR GOALS

Business strategies are the activities that will be undertaken to achieve the goals. You will also need to develop your point of differentiation, your uniqueness, and your *competitive advantage*.

Determine your competitive advantage

Business gurus argue that each business should be aware of its competitive advantage. For a consultant this may be a little difficult to define, as there may well be a full page of, say, trainers or engineers in the *Yellow Pages* for your area. Most elite professional firms claim it is 'their people', 'their service' or their 'tailored solutions' that afford them their distinctiveness. Clients who hear these clichéd phrases from all their suppliers naturally become sceptical.

A practical way of expressing what is different and unique about your service is to reflect on what people say when they praise you. This gives you an insight into what you should offer as your differentiator, what is unique about you.

A secondary aspect of uniqueness is the fact that you are there talking with the prospect and you know what they want; you also know their business. They know these things and that you are offering the service they want. This may well be enough for them to want you now! However, let's get back to the planning stage.

Some examples of consultants' competitive advantage are:

- Theresa the relocations specialist: pays attention to detail and knows her city intimately. She has excellent contacts in the real estate business, enabling her to locate prestige rental properties for her clients' occupancy. Theresa has a network so she can provide her services in all Australasian cities.
- Brian the combustion and explosives consultant who is also a professor emeritus: knows his area of specialisation as well as anyone in the English-speaking world, has extensive 'expert witness' experience and is a regular contributor to international forums.
- Glenda the management trainer: has a warm, friendly and helpful approach and guarantees outstanding evaluations from course participants.
- James the computer consultant: will attend at your house or your office and will see you on weekends or at night. James is always available (unless he is with another client)!

Select the strategies

Getting back to the strategies, here is a list that prospective consultants could consider. I use this as an audit list when coaching consultants in their businesses.

Marketing strategies

1. Spend at least one day a week marketing your services. If you are a contractor, you should devote half a day a week, on average, to this aspect. Do not leave your marketing until your current engagement finishes.
2. Develop a list of products and write them up as one-page A4 flyers.
3. Be careful with this one as many who develop this strategy sound false. It is to develop succinct 'client benefit statements' about what you do, so the client can see that you may be useful. Try to express what you do in words that imply a benefit to the client yet are in a 'fair dinkum' Australasian context. Examples of this are:
   - The maintenance engineer who says 'I work with plant machinery. What I do is I maintain it to keep it working reliably and I look after it so that its productive life is extended'.
   - The bookkeeper who says 'I work with small and medium businesses in the office. I keep financial records up to date, and basically look after those compliance aspects like BAS, tax, Workcover etc. I help my clients avoid fines and let them get on with what they like doing'.
   - The freelance photographer who says 'I make you look ravishingly beautiful (handsome), interesting, alluring . . .'

   In each of these cases, you need to be able to prove your claims. Otherwise you sound like you are unduly influenced by a half-baked spruiker who lacks practical experience with real Aussies and Kiwis!
4. Develop a profile in the marketplace as a specialist.

Client-type strategies

1. Seek out successful clients. They are always looking for new ideas. They are usually happier to pay, because they can afford it, and are more likely to have a positive record in dealing with consultants.
2. Seek out larger clients, as they have more locations, more people and therefore bigger assignments. They will engage you for more days. Additionally, the managers who hire you, unlike those in small business, are not spending their own money. They are spending the corporation's money or the budget allowance.

– Identify, secure and maintain as clients three major clients who are each capable of engaging you to the extent of 10 per cent of your target level of income.

– Identify, secure and maintain as sub-major clients five who are each capable of engaging you to the extent of 5 per cent of your target level of income.

3. Seek repeat business, as that should be the easiest to win.

Behaviour strategies

1. Be visible: make personal contacts. Go and see people, have coffee or lunch with them. If you leave all your contact to the written word, communicating only by email or letters, you will be at a disadvantage compared with those who use live marketing techniques.

2. Follow up all marketing and other client letters with phone calls to ensure that they have been received and are actioned.

3. Stay in touch with your networks and stay in touch with all clients, ideally at least on a 90-day basis. Structure your contacts so that they are useful to the client rather than being in the way or bothersome.

4. Continually market, because everyone is your advocate. After you have done a job and the client has the chance to make a referral, they become your advocate. If they make the referral, that is positive advocacy; if they say nothing, that is neutral advocacy; if they speak against you, that is negative advocacy. Whichever way, they are your advocate.

Leverage strategies

1. Leverage off the professional associations and industry bodies to which your clients belong. Do this by speaking at their conferences or running programs for their members. If you are not a speaker or a trainer then write for their journals and newsletters. This will build your profile, enhance your credibility, give exposure to your clients and possibly earn you fee income.

2. Leverage off your associates. Create some synergy with like-minded and complementary service providers so that you can bid for larger projects, deputise for one another when unavailable and thus keep clients 'in-house' so that they are less likely to go to your competition.

Financial strategies

1. Set non-financial goals and targets for activity levels in your business to have measures of success other than income earned. This is very important in the early stages of your consultancy as it may take some time for the business to be built.
2. Always sell to your competence rather than on a price basis. Being competitive on price will be more of an issue for contractors than for consultants and freelancers. However, all must be aware of relative value on offer to the client.

Management strategies

1. Have a mentor, manager, supervisor or co-director who is involved in what you are doing and who ensures that the goals and action plans you are setting are completed, met, and regularly reviewed and renewed.
2. Look for people to be your sponsors in organisations where you are engaged. These people will be your champions. They will recommend you and help ensure that your service delivery is successful.
3. Seek to get rated as a preferred supplier for your prospects, then find out the thresholds for obtaining three prices or for going to tender. Structure your proposals appropriately and bid under these limits so that you are in a competitive position less often.
4. Persist. Nothing beats persistence.

9. CREATE YOUR ACTION PLAN

In this section you detail exactly what you will do in the next period, your first 90 days, to market and implement your goals and to develop your business, step by step. A typical action plan follows, detailing:

- what is to be done;
- by whom it is to be done (in this case you assume it will be by you);
- when it is to be done by; and
- with what resources (including estimated expenditure).

Typical action plan

Month/task	Action (assuming 1 January start-up)	Date	Resources	Done
1.1	Prepare promotional materials	30/1	Old CV, designer, $1000	
1.2	Prepare list of 150 prospects—or warm suspects. If you do not have them you will need to do some mass marketing and/or telemarketing	30/1	Old CV, web search, call old colleagues	
1.3	Network, cultivate contacts: have coffee/ lunch with 4 contacts, ring total of 12 contacts	30/1	Marketing plan. $20 per lunch, $6 per coffee meeting	
1.4	Network, cultivate contacts: attend 2 net- work meetings, and one PD seminar	30/1	Check AIM & other bodies. Allow $40 per seminar	
1.5	Give positive messages: 'Going well, enjoying it . . .'	Constantly practise		
1.6	Go to the coast on a warm day and see old friends, spread the word: 'Going well, enjoying it . . .'	31/1	Plan the day	
2.1	Get website up and functioning: $500 design, $150 domain registration and $300 hosting	3/2	Marketing kit: $950 in full year	
2.2	Contact 20 prospects by mail	10/2	Marketing kit and an offer	

Month/task	Action (assuming 1 January start-up)	Date	Resources	Done
2.3	Ring those 20 prospects	17/2	List	
2.4	Arrange 5 interviews/ meetings with prospects	28/2	Marketing kit including samples of work; check prospects' websites	
2.5	Continue to network, cultivate contacts, give positive messages: 5 lunches/coffees in February. Two industry activities: meetings or workshops	28/2	Consult list of prospects in marketing plan	
2.6	Target 2 speaking/ writing engagements	28/2	Marketing plan	
2.7	Receive invitations to put proposals to 3 prospects, or at least referrals to 4 other interested prospects	7/3	To be revealed in interviews with prospects	
3.1	Contact 10 prospects by mail	21/3	Marketing plan	
3.2	Ring those 10 prospects	31/3	Marketing plan, scripts	
3.3	Arrange interviews with 4 prospects	10/4	Marketing plan	
3.4	Receive invitations to put proposals to 2 prospects	20/4	In interviews	
3.5	Get 3 referrals from prospects	20/4	From interviews	
3.6	Secure 2 speaking/ writing engagements	20/4	From interviews, marketing kit	

Month/task	Action (assuming 1 January start-up)	Date	Resources	Done
3.7	Continue to network, cultivate contacts, give positive messages: 3 lunches/coffees, one industry meeting	30/4	As per marketing plan	
3.8	Get 2 jobs—to start either this month or the next	30/4	From interviews, phone	

Now that you have completed your initial planning process, it will be a straightforward task to write up your business plan. Refer to the previous discussion to help you write up each item.

THE PARTS OF A WRITTEN BUSINESS PLAN

1. INTRODUCTION
This will comprise your vision, values and mission statement, which you prepared as part of the planning process.

2. THE BUSINESS
In this section you move from the broader concepts into more concrete aspects of your planning, addressing the following issues.

Activities
This section lists the activities of the business and how they are conducted. For example, a bookkeeper will keep books and prepare financial reports, and do so either on the clients' premises or from their own office.

Goals (or objectives)
You have prepared these goals as part of your planning process. They are the outcomes you want to achieve in the specified periods. It is usual for

a plan to cover three years with a yearly breakdown. The plan is revised at least annually, but ideally on a quarterly basis.

Competitive advantage

You have also prepared this as part of the planning process. Competitive advantage is an evolving notion, however; after you have won some engagements and received feedback from your clients it will become clearer why they have engaged you, and your understanding of your competitive advantage will become stronger.

Key success factors

Also identified in the planning process, your KSFs will be listed in this part of the plan for continual review and to remind you of them as you operate your business.

3. STRATEGY

This is the direction you will pursue to achieve your goals. It might be that you will concentrate on doing compliance work with in-house delivery for clients in the petroleum industry. For another consultant, the strategic direction might be to concentrate on providing a range of human resources management services to SMEs that do not have their own HRM personnel.

Strategy is often essentially a statement about your areas of specialisation. The activity, or the various activities, in which you specialise is essentially what you do. You may also have an industry specialisation in which you perform these services. Finally, some consultants have a regional specialisation in the location where they operate.

4. MARKETING PLAN

Your marketing plan is effectively the six Ps of the marketing mix which are fully described in Chapter 7 as Step 3 (see pages 142–9). You simply give the detail for those points. The research you have conducted, and your analysis of the market, would be contained in your plan. You should also detail the marketing strategies you use, and information about the target market in terms of its size, its potential and influential factors.

If you detail what you will do for each of the six Ps, you will have effectively developed your production plan as well as the marketing plan.

5. FINANCIAL INFORMATION

In this section you endeavour to calculate the financial needs of your business, particularly in the first year. It may well take six months to become cash-flow positive, that is, to earn more than you are spending. Some businesses take a year to achieve profitability. The longer it takes, the greater and more frequent is the need to revisit your strategy. You should also consider taking advice from your support group of consultants.

To calculate your cash flow, you will need to estimate how much you will need for capital purposes, that is, to acquire the items you need at the start of your business. You can do this by working through the list in Chapter 6. You will also need to quantify the amount you spend on current items—that is, regularly recurring expenses such as energy and telephone bills, travel and general office expenses. These items are also listed in Chapter 6. These two categories comprise the outflow of funds.

There also needs to be an estimate of the likely inflow of funds from fees for the sale of your services. It is probable that in the first six to twelve months inflow will be less than outflow. In these conditions, some alternative source of finance will be necessary. The possibilities here include:

- Savings from previous employment, separation allowance (redundancy payment), superannuation or sale of assets. You could call this equity finance because it is funds that you already own.
- Income from continuing employment for you and/or your partner.
- Some form of borrowing. The lowest cost loans tend to be home equity loans, where you borrow against the security of your own home and are able to draw down and repay with great flexibility, paying only for the money that you actually borrow at an interest rate that is close to the rate for owner-occupied home loans. Personal loans tend to be more expensive.

Irrespective of the comprehensiveness of your planning, you will need to make plans for the availability of cash to meet your everyday requirements for living, as distinct from running the business. This will come from the same sources.

In addition to cash-flow forecasts, a comprehensive plan will show when it is anticipated that the venture will become profitable. If you are to seek finance from a bank or other financial institution, they will be interested to see when you plan to become profitable. An adviser with financial expertise should be able to prepare documents showing your full financial details.

It is currently normal practice for people in business to commit as much of their expenditure as possible to credit cards, providing they are responsible with the use of credit. This is usually all payments other than to staff, landlords, financial institutions and the Tax Office. In doing so, card users accumulate many frequent flyer points. Providing the card is paid off each month, there may be considerable benefits to you such as extended credit and free travel.

6. MANAGEMENT AND STAFFING

It is common for those who trade as sole operators to forget that they are actually a business, with different roles to be performed and managed. While the blur factor will mean that you are a little unclear at the planning stage, it is a good idea to assign certain tasks to certain roles in your plan, and for you in the first instance to perform them.

As your business grows you can delegate these functions to the appropriate person. Many small business people endeavour to learn bookkeeping. If you have little aptitude for the systematic approach needed to keep financial records, however, you would be working smarter if you pass this task on to another service provider and use your time to find new clients or to stay in touch with existing ones.

It is worthwhile considering setting up some form of advisory panel for your business. Where a company has its board of directors, you could have an advisory panel. This does compromise the confidentiality of your activities but a trusted adviser or two can be of invaluable assistance. Often your partner will default to this role, as you will tend to tell them what goes on in the course of everyday activities.

7. STRUCTURE AND SUPPORT

This section will include the structure of your organisation, the type of business vehicle (sole proprietor, partnership or company), your location, and your business advisers and suppliers (lawyer, accountant, bookkeeper, banker and any other key suppliers).

It may be to your advantage to select key suppliers and develop some form of relationship with them. This is just practising what you will most likely preach. If you place most or all of your business with key suppliers, they will be more likely to help you with free advice, special offers and preference in delivery—you can jump to the top of the queue. I have long had such an arrangement with my computer consultant, who is also a supplier of hardware and software and is an Internet service provider (ISP). I have had a similar arrangement with the two accountants I have used.

These suppliers may also become your advocates and you in turn will probably advocate that others use their services.

8. SUPPORTING DOCUMENTS

All legal documents including leases, contracts and letters of engagement should be retained. If you apply for finance, the lending official will want to inspect them.

If you have a unique process that you have created yourself, you should consider having it patented or at least give it a registered trademark. As you take the new idea into the marketplace it will become known and others may try to adopt it as their own, or even register it as their own. Further advice about this should be obtained from a lawyer or patent attorney specialising in this field.

9. ACTION PLANS

In this section you detail exactly what you will do in the next period to market and implement your goals, and to develop your business. This is shown in full detail earlier in this chapter.

Key points

- Write up a plan—four pages will do. It is a dynamic document to be continually modified in the light of changes to the environment.
- The business plan is used to give you direction. You won't need to spend a couple of hours each morning working out what to do—you implement the plan.
- Developing a vision of where you want to be will help through any lean times.
- Being clear about your values will allow you to decide much earlier about whether an opportunity is worthwhile pursuing, and whether you want to be involved with people you meet on your journey.
- Having clearly defined and measurable goals will help you work more effectively.
- Formulate your competitive advantage. That is, know why people engage you. It will help people to see what you can do for them, and it will boost your confidence when describing what you can do for clients.
- By identifying the key success factors for your business, you can readily focus on what is important.
- Develop relationships with clients, particularly larger clients who regularly engage consultants.
- Be prepared to write up two versions of your plan: one for the financier should you need to borrow some money; the other for your everyday functioning, which you can review quarterly.

4

ESTABLISHING YOUR OFFICE

Who's the odd one out?

- President of the United States
- Prime Minister of Britain
- Premier of New South Wales
- the Pope
- Ian Benjamin (author of this book).

And the answer is, the Premier of New South Wales. Reason? All the others work from home.

Establishment is an exciting time, as it will have a large impact on your lifestyle for the foreseeable future. In choosing the site for their office, most consultants consider three main alternatives:

- at home
- an office in a business district
- a shared office with complementary types.

Access to Internet technology, the availability of lower-cost office supplies and the mobile telephone have combined to make it very easy to work independently, whether from home or from an external office.

WHY HAVE YOUR OFFICE AT HOME?

More than a million Australians work from home.[1] A far greater number have home offices to bring work home to or to pursue a hobby. There are many excellent reasons for having your office at home. Let's start by considering these.

A major advantage is that having a home office gives you the flexibility to change the focus or the size of your business without the constraints of leases on offices. When starting out in your own business, it is normal to be a little blurred about what lies ahead. Some years ago I formed my own financial advisory business, only to be offered a job in a merchant bank that was too good to knock back. The setting-up process had just finished when I had to dismantle the business, release my assistant and assign the lease to a new tenant. If you decide working for yourself is not for you, those with home offices will have minimum downsizing activity!

The second major advantage is that providing you have room at home, you can save money by not having to pay commercial rent. Many consultant businesses are cash-flow negative in the first six months— you can expect to trade at a loss. Some people with one or two major jobs lined up go into business for themselves on the strength of those opportunities. Initially the cash flow is very good, as they are working at rates which provide a return in excess of their former hourly rate as employees. However, when these contracts are completed the cash flow is likely to dry up, as their client base is a little thin, and the financial discipline necessary for small business will then become apparent. Having your office at home can represent a saving of between $5000–$15 000 a year, depending upon the amount of space, the prestige of your location and the amount of services available to you as a tenant.

A third major advantage of having your office at home is that you can work when there is work to do and when your effectiveness is optimal. You can adopt more flexible working hours. Some of us are owls: we work very effectively late into the night. Others are larks: at their best around dawn and in the early hours of the day. If there is no work to do you can use the time profitably to do other things. If you are tired in the heat or lull of the afternoon—take a nap.[2] The rituals of travel and office protocol are dispensed with, so productivity gains can occur in this area as well. Work on weekends if the weather is poor and get out midweek for a walk or sport when the weather is sunny.

Lifestyle is an important aspect for many starting their own businesses. The home office is often a major aspect of the plan. It provides an excellent opportunity to make a major change. You can be closer to your family or partner. If you spend a lot of the day at client premises, you will probably need to spend time in your office at night. If your office is not at home, this will not be good for relationships and may not be part of your planned lifestyle improvement. Having the office at home partly overcomes this drawback of the consultant's lifestyle. Home offices also allow you the benefits of minimal travel and working when you want to work. You may also be able to meet your desire to live in a preferred location—a coastal or country place perhaps.

In successfully working from home, you will be managing several issues.

CAN YOU MANAGE THE AT HOME/AT WORK CONTRADICTION?

Home is home to all the members of your family. It is where your friends visit, where your dog and cat sleep and where the children play. If you work from home you will always be at work and you will always be at home when you work. Young children may not understand that when you are at work in your home office you need privacy, to be able to talk to clients, to concentrate, to create and to engage prospective clients.

Spouses or partners may not understand the need for full professionalism in phone answering. Work is work, it is not romance! Great lovers can become task focused when they are earning their living. So the office is not only a separate room, it has a different atmosphere from the living room, let alone the bedroom. Similarly, you might like to make a transition when returning home from the office. If you have been highly focused, consider coming back into the family area via the post office or a walk around the block. Meet your partner or a friend for coffee down the street.

Lifestyle commentator Amanda Gore argues that work should not be taken to any part of the house that is important for other activities.

To do so will poison or pollute that room. American consultant Geoff Bellman says that if you put your office in your dining room, you will eat all your meals in front of the television; if you put it in your living room you will have friends over less often; if it is in the kitchen you will eat too many snacks.[3]

WILL YOU COPE WITH LOW ENERGY LEVELS AND LONELINESS?

In my experience the most overlooked aspect of working from home relates to the need to be continually motivated. The home office is usually an isolated one. It may be very quiet and devoid of peers creating action and group pressure. There are no weekly status reports or meetings to see how much work is in the pipeline, and no one is reviewing your business plan. Under these circumstances many consultants find it difficult to adjust to the otherwise salubrious atmosphere of the home office.

Extroverts get their energy from other people.[4] While they may be brilliant consultants, they may find it difficult to work in the isolated environment of the home office. They need to react with other people to be re-energised and productive.

Introverts on the other hand develop their energy themselves and do not need other people—they prefer their isolation. These people, however, may become too accustomed to being without people in their workplace. Their interpersonal skills may become so neglected that they find it difficult to make and sustain contacts at a suitable level.

To keep energy levels up and to overcome loneliness, it is important to network, attend meetings and give yourself rewards, perhaps by meeting friends at the end of the day. Use music, natural light, sunshine, exercise and the flexibility you have to your advantage so that you are constantly mindful of how lucky you are to be working from home.

CAN YOU AVOID CATCHING 'SMALL HORIZONS SYNDROME'?

Goldfish grow when they are moved into a bigger bowl or into a garden pool. They adjust to their larger surroundings. Some consultants find the home office the equivalent of moving from the big pond into the little glass fishbowl.

It may be difficult to promote your leading-edge expertise if you are sitting in the third bedroom, waiting for the clothes drier to finish and watching the clock so you remember to pick the children up from school. You are still in your slippers and you are endeavouring to convince a CBD client of the need for your services. 'Small horizons syndrome' is the problem of shrinking your expectations about your capacity, feeling that you cannot do what you once did. The cause may be the limited perspective of a cramped little office with all sorts of domestic distractions.

Keeping in contact with like professionals and implementing a plan for your own development will help you flourish in your home office.

WHERE WILL YOU PUT YOUR HOME OFFICE?

One of the big pluses in owning and controlling your own business is that you can work from home. The technological capacity for consultants is abundant and affordable so it is possible now for you to live and operate where you want—which may mean leaving the big cities.

One consultant I know has his office in the loft above the old stables (now a garage) in Murrumbateman near Canberra. A couple who live and work as consultants on a property at Chiltern near Albury have sweeping views across thousands of hectares to the Rutherglen wine country. A business consultant at Runaway Bay on the Gold Coast looks out over a canal and his boat. Robert in Cairns sees the rainforest from between the slats on his windows on his verandah in his charming old Queenslander home.

In the cities, Michael in South Perth has a panoramic outlook over the Swan River from his office in his apartment. Jan looks straight down Sydney Harbour from her attic office in Mosman.

I am now overlooking the Sunshine Coast and hinterland down to the coast and Maroochydore. For the previous six years I was in my Melbourne home office—north-facing, big sky views and a garden featuring a huge oak tree, which was always moving and always changing. Prior to that I was in a garden bungalow, which also worked well. I have met hundreds of home workers who have neat or messy offices in their dining rooms, spare bedrooms and garages.

One of the first issues to be addressed in setting up a home office is the matter of local government regulations.

LOCAL GOVERNMENT COMPLIANCE REQUIREMENTS

Consultants use their intellectual capacity and considerable experience in helping clients in their businesses. As such we tend not to hold stock nor produce noxious goods nor have customers traipsing into our residences. You may have a bookkeeper or word-processing consultant attend, but be prepared to ask them to do your work at their office. This would be the case if the entrance to your own home office was in any respect 'high risk'. Steep inclines, potentially aggressive dogs and dark or obscure access could all be classified as high risk for these purposes.

When you inquire from your local government about its regulations, make clear what you anticipate will be the level of business traffic. It may well be zero. Different municipalities have differing requirements.

The areas that you will need to find out about are:

* permits or licences to conduct a business from home
* parking requirements
* any other special rules.

INSURANCE REQUIREMENTS

In the event that anyone does attend your home office on a business matter, you will need to check that your public liability domestic policy covers any situation where the visitor may be able to sue you for negligence; for example, a tile or some other object falls off your roof and hits them on the head.

You will also need to check if your home insurance policy covers the items that are used in your business against damage or loss from fire and theft. The rules that apply to consultants who are sole traders may be different to the ones that apply to those who are proprietary limited companies. It is not possible for me to be prescriptive here, as there is a large number of insurance companies and an even larger range of insurance policies. Irrespective of what you are told by the officer of an insurance company, do check to confirm what they say when you receive written information about the policies. This is generally available on the Internet so it is easy to access.

Workcover, or insurance against misfortune from accidents or misadventure while you are at work, varies from state to state. You will also need to check what your situation is and make sure that the cover you take out applies to your mode of operation. The rules are different for companies and for sole traders.

LEASE CONDITIONS IF YOU LIVE IN RENTED PREMISES

The body corporate of an apartment complex will have rules for insurance and for activities that can lawfully be conducted on the premises. There may also be rules for visitors, parking and issues about access to the Internet that will need to be addressed. Clarify these issues before you decide that you will operate from home when home is an apartment with a body corporate.

When you are satisfied that there is no regulatory limitation on your home office, and you have satisfied the requirements that do exist, what are the factors you need to consider when creating that special space? Let's look at the fundamentals.

WHAT REALLY MAKES A HOME OFFICE WORK?

The information which appears here is distilled from hundreds of conversations with consultants over many years. These are aspects to look for when you create your home office. Most of them apply to external offices as well.

PRIVACY

Out of the way and out of earshot of the rest of the home activities. Dogs and cats and noisy children all present an unprofessional image to callers. So do partners or spouses who have trouble answering the telephone in the business name. Clearly there is a need for a separate business telephone line. Have a separate place for your office. It should be beyond the range of noises from television, children, dishwashers, dogs and cats and anything else domestic! Have clear rules about who comes into the office and when they may do so. This applies to young children and perhaps to friends who are regular visitors.

The 'friends who call in' issue is one of the most significant distractions for consultants working from home. You are always at home and therefore can always be visited. That's what some good friends seem to think!

It is a good idea to endeavour to keep work inside the office. Special projects may extend to the dining room from time to time but by keeping things neat and cleaning up the table each night, the sanctity of your home can be preserved.

BRIGHT, SUNNY, WITH A VIEW

Anything else is a little depressing. This is of acute importance if you are extroverted in nature and therefore derive energy from other people. Trees, bushes and shrubs constitute a view. The sky can also be a great view.

SPACE

You will need adequate space for your current project. Working with too little space (and with no view) can lead to the development of 'small horizons syndrome'. It was noted earlier that goldfish grow when they are moved into a larger environment. I wonder what happens to them when they are moved back into the bowl from the garden pond. I think they might die!

AVAILABILITY OF MUSIC

Music can be an energy source. It is also mood changing. The massage rooms in the therapeutic springs at Daylesford or the Blue Mountains or Montville all have rainforest or ocean tapes playing to relax their clients. High profiler speakers use tracks from the Superman theme or other stirring compositions to boost anticipation for their performances. Australia and New Zealand are well served with classical FM networks which provide reasonably continuous music during the day. The morning and late afternoon programs can be excellent background music and a source of added energy! There is a host of music stations on the Internet and among the public broadcasters. There is always the SBS test pattern, your MP3 player and your own collection of CDs.

AMBIENCE

Create a good atmosphere in your office. If the office looks and feels right, you will be able to work. If it is not right, productivity will be lower. The 'look and feel' concept is an abstract one but you will know it when you sit down to get your business up and running. It may well be that the look and feel is the combination of the previous factors— light, views, etc. To get the feel right you could consider using an interior designer or do it yourself. If you choose the latter, spend some time considering what it is that you like in a room and then seek to translate that feel into your office.

WOULD AN EXTERNAL OFFICE SUIT YOU BETTER?

Many smaller businesses have surplus space in their offices and are happy to sublet a portion to someone they trust, who will pay them some rent and who may bring some extra clients, skills or just a brighter personality to their workplace.

For two years I had an office in a small legal firm where the lawyer was a sole practitioner; we enjoyed discussing the events of the world, business and client relationships. There was some cross-referral of clients but the main benefit for him was my weekly contribution to his rent.

If anyone were to visit my premises, this set-up did look good. I was often approached by other independents wanting to do joint ventures. Clients were not invited to my office but the joint venturers were. They were impressed with my professional suite but, realistically, such premises do look very small scale!

Other minor benefits to the independent in an external office are access to professional phone answering if required, access to photo-copiers, scanners and other such equipment that one may not have.

The external office can be excellent for confidentiality and it leaves home as a haven rather than a workplace.

Serviced offices offer a range of services including phone answering, mailing, reception and access to an office, for periods varying from a few set hours up to full time. There is some contact with like-minded professionals working on a small scale, but investigation reveals that these are relatively expensive for what you receive.

It could also be argued that the office in the prime CBD location is a mild form of deception, but most people in business will recognise it for what it is. Some serviced offices are in the most expensive office buildings in the city. They even have the top floor as their location. It is my contention that this fools very few people. It is apparent that the consultant is a consultant—operating solo. Why then do they have this office in the best building in the city? Obvious answer—it is a serviced office!

Serviced offices suit those who have many new clients, particularly those in human resources and recruitment. They can also have the image of being CBD or near-CBD. They are also good for the extro-vert, good when you lack space at home and very good as an interim step on your way to your own office.

MAYBE YOU COULD SET UP A BUSINESS VILLAGE?

In the inner suburb of Armadale in Melbourne, a group of construction and design industry consultants conduct their businesses from a converted church. A mezzanine platform has been built to utilise the vaulting height of the building.

Around the walls on both levels there are desks made of flush-panel doors resting horizontally on two-drawer filing cabinets. The doors make great desktops as they are just over two metres in length and about 80 centimetres wide, providing plenty of workspace. Other doors rest on A-frame trestles. It all looks very elegant, which can perhaps be attributed to the design sensibilities of the users. The striking visual image is a juxtaposition of order and creativity, attention to detail and awareness of cost. It also gives a strong message of professionalism to the clients of these businesses.

A dozen firms operate from the old church. They include project managers, architects, draftspeople, surveyors, designers, town planners, interior decorators and building inspectors. There is also an office service located in the building that performs telephone answering, word processing and plan printing, and has a range of office equipment including a scanner, fax, photocopier and binding machine for the use of tenants.

In the old goldmining area of Creswick near Ballarat, a similar business village has been established in an old shed. It looks just like any old shed from the road but around the back it has a fully glassed wall opening to a broad area of decking. This overlooks north-facing slopes down to a river. There is ample car parking in the shade of large eucalypts. The consultants who use these offices service agriculture, local government and community groups.

In Newcastle a group of consultants who used to work for BHP occupy a large warehouse formerly used by their old employer. They loosely associate from time to time on projects as the opportunity arises. They were also the beneficiaries of arrangements made when they left BHP that gave them a certain amount of work over the next two years. They found that working under the one roof provided great synergy and energy that has seen them develop teamwork which clients have appreciated. As most tenders are won by groups rather than individuals, they are also in a good position to capitalise on their skills and contacts to win tender business.

This business village has been established for years and some of the original occupants have gone on to build their own larger businesses.

Variations on this theme are many. In Canberra a group of mainly ex-army people work from the garage of one. It is large and very well appointed. The two principals have a team of up to 60 independents who are located across Australia. They offer a broad range of management consulting services. The business was started over fifteen years ago and is, by the measures of reputation, client quality, scale of operations and financial criteria, very successful.

These office options all have the advantage that the energy levels of the participants are higher as they bounce off one another. They share resources, infrastructure and information. They go to work in a friendly professional environment which is at a very reasonable cost to them. They also have the advantage that home remains home and should be more restful and harmonious.

Participants in these shared offices also have more opportunities to work in teams on larger projects, like the Canberra consultants mentioned above. There is some cross-referral activity and they are all better placed to syndicate for tenders and larger contracts.

Business village offices have the advantage of accommodating client visits, which is rarely an option for home-based businesses. Mind you, in the professional services areas, few new clients come to the home office: you tend to meet them at their premises or in coffee shops or hotels.

Consultants who work in shared offices may develop a more outward-looking and growth-oriented perspective as the environment is always business like rather than homely.

Shared offices with related professionals are well suited to industries where team approaches are common. They are more likely to be found in construction and engineering, the arts, counselling, education, and financial and legal professional services.

The trade-off in these situations is some loss of confidentiality about client base; because it is not your own space, decisions have to be made involving sharing and concessions. Working at odd hours can sometimes be difficult.

WHAT EQUIPMENT IS NEEDED?

Most of you will already have what is necessary to equip an office for a consultant. You will need some space to put work things. Filing cabinets can be archive boxes from the major office suppliers. (If you choose an external office you will need to arrange for additional printers, Internet and fax access and standard furniture, including a good chair, a desk and filing cabinets.)

Next on the list is a telephone that is answered as a business phone. That is, between the hours of 8 am and 6 pm it should be answered in a way that makes the caller think they have rung a business number, no matter who answers it. When you leave the office, it is best if the caller can still catch you, immediately, so best practice would see you divert the landline to your mobile phone when you are out. It is often too late if you wait until the end of the day, when you return to the office, to hear the messages and it may not be possible for others to pass them on during the day. The mobile also allows you to make contact with clients as soon as is possible. Promote your mobile as your major business phone by putting its number on your business card and elsewhere in bold format and above or before the landline, which should be in smaller normal font. Do have a positive message on your voicemail encouraging callers to leave a message and do return these calls as soon as possible.

After the space, the desk and the phones, the home office needs a computer. The portability of the notebook can greatly enhance your productivity. You may also have a desktop but it is good to have all your files on the one server—your own notebook perhaps. The printer is essential, as is Internet access.

So in summary: office, desk, chair, filing cabinets, telephone, mobile, PC, printer. A scanner, photocopier and binding machine may be necessary for some consultants but these services are generally widely available. Often it is a lack of space which prevents an office from having all these tools.

Items for consideration for a home office

Item	Priority	Cost estimate	Comment
Telephone	High	$5 pcm to $100	
Mobile telephone	High	'free' to $500	Voicemail essential. Avoid low coverage networks
Answering machine	Low	$80	Only to be used as a back-up if you forget to divert your phone to your mobile
Broadband modem	High	$50 pcm	
Wireless router	Medium	$150	Nice to have
Notebook PC	High	$2000	Buy the latest as it's a moving target
Desktop PC	Low	$1000	Use funds for hard-drive back-up device
Laser printer	High	$400	Laser for quality printing. Many non-laser printers have soluble print
3-in-1 colour printer/ scanner/photocopier	High	$90	Great value
Fax machine	Medium	$300	Useful, not essential 24/7. Make number available 'on request'
Caller ID machine	Medium	$40	Shows the phone number of callers (unless caller has pre-selected anonymity) which lowers stress levels as you can recognise frequently called numbers before answering

Item	Priority	Cost estimate	Comment
Desk + filing cabinets	High	$40 + 2 × $150	Try a flush-panel door resting on two 2-drawer filing cabinets, or a trestle from Ikea or Freedom
Chair	High	$150	Buy a good one
Step files	High	$12	Place the work in progress files in these: next job first. You can view 8 files at once
Box for desktop implements	High	$20	Keep the desktop clear, place items in filing cabinets, drawers or in this plastic box
File storage & bookshelves	High	$300	Portable shelving allows for flexibility and coupled with lever-arch files provides for good client file access. Filing cabinets are still great value although heavy to move. Buy new ones, they work better!

Three good ways to save money when setting up your office are:

- The filing cabinet or Ikea trestle combination with a flush-panel door. This saves up to $2000 on a new desk and even more on installation costs.
- Buy the three-in-one colour printer, scanner and copier and go to the print shop for important jobs.
- Forgo an answering machine and always divert your desk phone to your mobile.

ARE HOME OFFICES PROFESSIONAL?

The unprofessional tag becomes less pertinent each year. There are differences in certain business sectors, but for the consultants reading this book the home office is rarely seen as a disadvantage. Why?

Most consultants will go to the client's premises. You tend not to meet clients, either new or old ones, at your home offices.

A consultant is chosen for a job primarily because the client antici-pates that you will do the job well and at a more reasonable price than the provider who is in the best building in the city with large overheads.

You are often out of your office—working with the client on site or at their offices. At very busy times you may only get into your office on the weekend or at night. If you have your office at home you may find that you can spend a little more time with your family, possibly placating a significant other who would be even less impressed if you had to spend catch-up time at an office away from home.

Here are a few principles that I have found useful in addressing the issue of the professionalism of the office of the consultant, whether at home or external:

- Be positive in your attitude and appearance at all times.
- Always answer the telephone in a professional manner—both live answering and on voicemail. Give a greeting, the name of your business and then your name. Avoid adding the redundant 'speaking' after your name.
- Ensure that you have a separate telephone line for business.
- Have quality letterheads and business cards: professionally designed, up to date without any alterations; the letterhead should be on 90 gsm paper or heavier.
- Sign up for a commercial email address (one you pay for). Free email addresses often have restrictions on the amount of infor-mation that can be received. Clients may also have doubts about the confidentiality of their business if you use a free email address.
- If you are a high profiler consultant, or if you have many clients because your engagements are of a short-term nature, you will look more professional if you have a website. Your own domain would be

appropriate if you are earning high fees, or if you work in the IT industry.

- Your address at 15 Primrose Crescent, Suburbia may not matter. If it does (because it's in a totally different socio-economic segment from the addresses of your clients) there are ways of disguising your real address. You can rent an address—perhaps at your accountant's office or at some other serviced office in your area, or in a business area. This will give you a different fax number and different phone numbers. You can also have a post office box, which usually costs less than $50 a year—a dollar a week.

If you have a business-like email address, professional business card and letterhead and a telephone which is always answered in a business-like manner, the client may consider the post office box address to be very efficient.

Economising on these items may indicate to your clients that you are likely to take short cuts, that you are happy with second best, and that near enough is good enough. It also suggests under-investment in your business systems.

Key points

- Practise professionalism and be business-like, particularly when you work from home.
- As individuals, you have differing preferences for how you like to work. Some people need to go to a real office building, wear a suit and maybe even have a secretary. Others like a laptop, an open-neck shirt and a view over the water. Any permutation is possible.
- In my case I always wanted to work from home. While reasonably extroverted, I like to work by myself. I have proved I can do it. The corollary to this is that I am not good at working in teams. I notice this characteristic with some of my close associates, and we often talk about this factor—that our strength is also our weakness.
- Shared offices and business villages have great advantages—but someone has to do the organisation. Perhaps this is an opportunity for you?
- Working with others will see a higher level of energy in the workplace, more frequent creation of ideas and opportunities for joint venturing.
- The home office, in summary, has the following advantages and disadvantages:

Advantages	Disadvantages
• Low cost	• Less professional
• Flexible	• Constraints of space
• Short lease	• Distractions
• See more of family	• More interruptions
• Your house may have a better view than your office	• Lonely—low energy—lack of motivation
• Save time on travel	• Lack of stimulus for creativity
• Air is cleaner	• 'Small horizons syndrome'
• Work at any time	• Casual employees have to come into your home
• Work when you really feel like it	

5

ESTABLISHING YOUR BUSINESS

There are four types of business vehicles in which consultants may operate. These are the sole trader or sole proprietor, the partnership, the company and the trust. The first two are classified as unincorporated; the company is a corporation (incorporated); and the trust is effectively represented by a trustee, which is either an individual or company. All businesses need an ABN (Australian Business Number). It is best to apply for the ABN as soon as you have chosen your business structure and the name for your business or company.

We shall apply a step-by-step approach to selecting the type of business vehicle, choosing its name and registering with all compliance aspects including the ABN, GST if appropriate, and with the ASIC.

STEP 1: SELECTING THE BUSINESS STRUCTURE

You have four choices for business structure—sole trader/sole proprietor, partnership, company or trust. There are advantages and disadvantages of each.

SOLE TRADER OR SOLE PROPRIETOR

This is the most common form of business vehicle for small business operators. It is the easiest, quickest and least costly form of operation to establish. As a sole proprietor you can trade under your own name and can start trading as soon as you obtain your ABN (see later in this chapter). To do this your business name must be your own name, unembellished. If you add *any* other words to your name, such as '& Associates', 'Consulting', 'Gardening Services' or 'Freelancing', you have a business name which should be registered. You can see how that is done in Step 2.

While the sole proprietorship form of operation is the quickest and least expensive to establish, it does have limitations.

First, many government entities and major businesses in Australia will not engage unincorporated consultants. The main reason for this is that there have been concerns that if unincorporated consultants do not pay themselves superannuation, the hirer may be liable for payment at some stage in the future.

Second, some hirers consider it administratively messy to engage unincorporated consultants. This is because they have chosen to make a number of separate payments to the Tax Office, a worker's compensation entity and a superannuation fund, and then the balance to the consultant. Other hirers are not concerned and are quite happy to pay the full sum to the unincorporated consultant.

There are two remedies available to you if you find yourself meeting this obstacle. The first is that many of these large corporations and government entities have established arrangements with the bigger consulting firms to facilitate the hiring of unincorporated contractors. For a fee, these firms sub-contract with the individual consultant and in turn contract with the hirer. The firms involved in such arrangements vary on the basis of where they are located, the activity they are involved in and the people who run them. It is a good idea to ask the hirer if they have such arrangements available to you if you find that this arises in discussion.

The second remedy is simply to incorporate. It may be easier and less costly overall to do this and it can be done quickly, as we see below.

PARTNERSHIP

The other form of unincorporated entity is the partnership. The major benefit of having a partnership is that the management, financial and physical burdens of running the business are shared. There may also be tax advantages, in that the income is shared between the partners.

A partnership agreement will need to be prepared for the parties, preferably by a lawyer who is their adviser. It will cover the following matters: the nature of the business, its purpose and how it will be managed, the roles and authority of the partners, responsibilities of the partners including the obligations to contribute financial resources, ownership and dispute resolution.

Another issue partnership members face is how to facilitate the exit of a partner from the business. A good way to deal with this issue is to plan for the exit at the time of formation of the partnership. If talks break down at this point you may have saved yourself a lot of heartache. You can imagine what might have happened in the event that you had gone ahead and developed a business together. Similarly, you need to plan for the potential admission of a new partner. The partnership agreement will also need to provide for its ultimate closure or dissolution, and the possible sale of the business name.

An important issue is the need to agree on the basis of remuneration of the members of the partnership. All partnerships will need to bring in new business and it is often the case that only some of the partners have this talent.

Related issues include how investment expenditure is funded, and the rights of the partners to the intellectual property created by the partnership. This may encompass the methodologies adopted in the delivery of service, products developed, the database and records of business transactions. The partnership agreement will also need to provide for changes to the hours worked by the partners and their rights and capacity to take time off.

A major disadvantage of this type of structure is that each partner is individually liable for all the debts of the business. A second disadvantage is the previously discussed reluctance of some government and corporate clients to do business with unincorporated entities.

Consulting and contracting lend themselves to doing joint ventures. It is relatively easy to form a joint venture for a particular purpose, after which the parties go their separate ways. Note, however, that high-profile consulting tends to be subject to reasonably rapid and constant change. The two partners who are a logical fit this year may have little relevance to each other by the end of next year.

Your accountant may have good reasons for you to either go into a partnership or stay out of one. These reasons may reflect the fact that there are special circumstances between the people contemplating the partnership. Either way, it is essential to have a partnership agreement drawn up by a lawyer who is a specialist in this area. This agreement will be the footings upon which your house of business is built. If there is no written prior agreement about how the partners in a business will ultimately part ways, then it will be by negotiation when the time comes. If the negotiations are unfruitful, the partners will then revert to the common law. This means they will resolve the matter by litigation. This would surely be an undesirable outcome from risk management, emotional and financial perspectives.

A PARTNERSHIP GONE WRONG

David and Phil had worked together for four years as mainten-ance engineers for a railways corporation. They were good friends and had complementary skills as maintenance service providers. They set up their own business in Sydney and it did well. They eventually won more work than they could handle and hired two more contractors on a needs basis.

Phil had excellent relationship management skills and as the business developed it was clear that all the new business came from Phil. In addition to his marketing function, he found he was spending more time on issues related to client relationships. Many of these related to his colleague's dealings with their clients. Eventually it became clear that he was the manager of the group and he did little maintenance work.

This trend continued and Phil was working more on weekends, planning the business growth. Ultimately Phil proposed to David that their partnership agreement needed revision as it had now evolved to be something much more elaborate and profitable than what they had first envisaged. Part of this revision, he suggested, would be an end to the 50/50 split of the profits of the partnership, unless he was also paid a salary three times that of a maintenance worker.

David did not accept this, arguing that Phil would not do the marketing without knowing that he had his reliable and skilled partner and friend David to deliver on all Phil's promises. Nine troubled months later, with thousands of dollars spent on lawyers' fees, the partnership was wound up and David and Phil were no longer friends. Phil has continued in a new business of his own. David decided to look for a job.

COMPANY

The third type of structure is the company. It is a separate legal entity and may provide some (but not complete) protection against adverse litigation. As a corporation, it can take legal action and in turn can also be sued.

Directors and managers of companies have been subject to increasingly stringent legislation and a more active regulatory regime. The degree of protection from litigation for company directors and for the providers of professional services is somewhat limited. The key issue is negligence; directors and managers of companies that provide professional services such as consulting and contracting need to adopt work practices that keep them up to date, that see them operating only in those areas where they have expertise; they need to protect their assets through professional indemnity insurance and/or by transferring their assets in some way on the advice of their lawyers.

The major advantage of a company for the consultant is the better positioning it gives you in the eyes of the market. It is seen as more business-like. For many hirers of consultants such as small businesses, not-for-profit organisations and householders, this will not be an issue, however.

The second major advantage is that anyone can hire you. The bar against unincorporated service providers discussed above does not apply.

Another major advantage of the company is the lower tax rate. In 2007 it is 30 per cent, and there is no minimum threshold. This lower tax rate allows some individuals to lower their tax by operating as a company; however, that benefit does not extend to consultants who earn their income through providing personal services. Personal services income is defined as the ordinary or statutory income of an individual that is primarily a reward for the individual's personal effort or skills.

To take advantage of the lower tax rate, irrespective of whether you carry on your business either as an individual or through an entity such as a company, certain tests must be satisfied. The most important test is the 'results test'. This means that at least 75 per cent of the income earned must be for producing a result, not just the supply of labour for an hourly rate. The individual is expected to supply any equipment and is liable to rectify any defective work. So to take advantage of any lower corporate (company) tax rate, the company needs to have an income stream from activities other than the sale of the consultant's time.

In practical terms this means that incorporated consultants should charge for deliverables other than their time. Examples of this include delivery of programs that have certain processes and outcomes or certain services provided rather than days taken to provide them.

Companies also allow more flexibility with carry-forward losses and with superannuation. It is recommended that you obtain your own advice as the tax and legal environment can change at any time. The budget process each year ensures that tax is reviewed at least once every year and case law can be developed daily by the courts. More information about tax and consultants appears later in this chapter.

Many new businesses choose to be a sole trader on the basis of set-up costs. In 2006, the Australian Government decreased its charge for incorporation from $800 to $400. This means you can now purchase your own company in Australia for about $550 by paying a $150 fee to Internet-based incorporators. Similarly, it may only cost $1200 per annum more to run a company for a small business; this includes the extra corporate regulator fees.

An accountant or a lawyer can arrange for you to set up a company. Accountants usually have greater awareness of the tax implications of the type of company structure you adopt and which may best suit your circumstances and aspirations. One option is to buy a shelf company. These are simply brand-new companies which no one has used before and are highly unlikely to have been owned by a corporate crook with hidden liabilities. Their name is due to the fact that they have been made in great numbers by specialist firms and are 'sitting on the shelf' in ring binders awaiting your collection. See the section below on 'How should you start?' to see how to acquire a shelf company.

TRUST

Trusts are seen to have two major advantages, but they may not apply to the service businesses described in this book. Many professional service providers place their assets in trusts as a risk management strategy in the event that they are ever successfully sued for professional negligence. The trust assets may be inaccessible for such creditors or litigants.

A second benefit of the trust is that it may allow for income to be distributed away from the principal income earner to other members of their family. Under current tax laws, income earned by professional service providers is generally termed 'personal services income' and as such cannot be redistributed to non-earners. Readers who wish to determine their individual situation should consult an accountant experienced in advising professional service providers.

HOW SHOULD YOU START?

Some of you will know you need to be a company. Your target market is major organisations. You are a high profiler and ambitious to earn a six-figure income. However, if you are uncertain about your new career in consulting, contracting or freelancing and uncertain about your commitment, start as a sole trader and be ready to incorporate if you need to to obtain the type of work you want.

If you are uncertain, don't let it show. If you want to run slowly and smell the roses, keep it to yourself. Clients want commitment from their service providers. Don't you?

You have chosen your business vehicle. You are now ready for the next step.

If you are going to incorporate and run as a company, then you could go to your accountant or to other specialist providers such as

<http://www.incorporator.com.au> or those listed in the *Yellow Pages*, and arrange for the purchase of a shelf company immediately.

STEP 2: CHOOSING YOUR NAME

For the independent service provider working from home, the choice of business name should be a relatively simple process. Why? As you are in a personal service business, presumably working by yourself and not really wanting to engage others, the best name is your own name. Here are some reasons why.

First, it is easier for people to remember how to get in touch with you if you market yourself under your own name. The proofreader who calls their business 'Proof Perfect' may be overlooked because the client cannot remember either the person's name or the business name.

Second, most business comes from people who know us—our network. By operating under our own name referrals get to us more quickly. People who don't know us can be sure that they have the right person, and overall brand awareness is greater. Conversely, if your market segment does not easily remember your name, for whatever reason, you would be wise to consider having a business name that is more recognisable.

Another important consideration is whether or not you can acquire the domain name for your business on the Internet. It is worthwhile checking to see whether someone else has registered the name. You can do this through a number of service providers. One is <http://www.conexim.com.au>; others are listed in the Resources section of this book. To see if the name you want is available, simply follow the easy steps on the appropriate page on that site.

IT'S ALL IN A NAME
In North Sydney there is a human resources consulting firm, run by Peter Armstrong, called Armstrong Miller and McLaren. The original office was at the corner of the prominent Miller and McLaren Streets in that suburb. This firm has prospered and now has a Melbourne office but the owner has resisted the

temptation to call it Armstrong Flinders and Collins. Notice how names that are familiar add substance, easier recognition and perhaps credibility to the name of the consultant's business.

An Adelaide consultant applied a similar strategy when he adopted the name Johnston Gordon & Walker. His surname was Johnston; the other two names were the second names of his two children. His reasoning for adopting Johnston Gordon & Walker was that it gave him greater substance in the clients' minds and that it was normal for professional advisers to operate under a combination of surnames. After a relatively short period he dropped the second and third names, as he felt uncomfortable when prospects questioned him about his associates.

Still in Adelaide, an engineering firm by the name of Forrest Davis & Smith changed its name to Forrest Davis & Bucholz. The reason? Partner Smith attended a summer MBA course at an American university. In a case study it was revealed that engineering firms had greater credibility with a German name in their title. Some years later the German name still stands—a successful strategy, it seems.

Another Sydney consultant adopted the acronym of his initials as his name (the initials stood for Alan Peter Edwards). APE Consulting scores high on recognition perhaps, but may be a little low on credibility!

Many people starting up as independents are attracted to acronyms as their business name. The reasons most commonly cited are relevance, recognition and flexibility, and the problem of naming is solved. The relevance part is that the initials of the person make up the acronym. It is hoped this gives recognition. The name does not restrict the service provider to any particular activity.

Another argument often advanced for acronyms is that many large organisations use them. However, the large organisations usually spend millions of dollars promoting the acronyms. They print them on literature which is widely distributed, and they place them on buildings in very prominent places in our cities. As small businesses, you cannot match this level of exposure and image building. On balance there is no compelling case for using an acronym.

NAMING WITH A VIEW TO SELLING YOUR BUSINESS

If you anticipate ever selling your business, then it is better to have a descriptive name which relates to some aspect of the business activity or area of specialisation.

As personal businesses are normally inseparable from the provider, it is often not easy to sell them. However, some people do, and in such circumstances the following things normally happen:

1. The sale takes place over a three-year period. During this time, the new purchaser is introduced as a partner of the vendor to the existing client base.
2. The purchase moneys are paid in a number of instalments over the three-year period. This is to assist in the retention of the existing customer base and in the business maintaining its initial agreed value.
3. With some notable exceptions, the outgoing consultant moves to a faraway place or retires from active practice.

If you wish to sell your business, it is best to advise your accountant as soon as you decide. Businesses with higher income and higher tax bills generally sell for more than businesses with lower income and lower tax bills.

ARE YOU READY TO CHOOSE THE NAME?

So, after consideration of all these factors, how does one go about choosing a name? Ask yourself these questions about your preferred name:

1. Does this name make it easier for my prospects to do business with me?
2. If I need to, can I use the name as my internet domain registration?
3. Does it support or enhance my credibility?
4. Is it easy to recognise as my business? Does it facilitate the promotion of good brand awareness?

Now is the time to choose your name. Think of about three or four names because the one you have chosen may have already been taken by someone else. To see if the name is already taken, go to the following Internet addresses:

- For a company: go to <http://www.asic.gov.au> and search the link to ASIC's National Names Index or use the ASIC Identical Names Check facility. Alternatively, you can go in person to any ASIC service centre, as listed in the Resources section.
- For a sole trader or partnership: to see if your preferred name is available, follow the links from <http://www.business.gov.au> for your particular state or territory. Alternatively, you can go to the relevant state government office nearest to you. The names of these appear in the Resources section.

As business names are a state responsibility, you will need to have the name registered in more than one state if you do not want someone in another state to copy it. Alternatively, if you incorporate and use that name as the company name, the company will own that name Australia-wide.

You have chosen your business name. You have already decided upon the type of business vehicle you want. It is now time for the next step.

STEP 3: DO YOU NEED TO REGISTER FOR GST?

An additional decision to be made at the set-up stage is whether or not to register for the GST (Goods and Services Tax). You will need to register for the GST if your annual income will be in excess of $50 000.

This means that you need to add 10 per cent to the fee component of your invoices. You will be able to claim back all the GST you pay on the goods and services that you have purchased for use in your business.

If you service the corporate sector, your customers can obtain a rebate for the GST they pay to you. If you provide services for households, as final consumers of goods and services they cannot obtain a rebate. Not-for-profit institutions and some government entities have different regulations applying and they can usually tell you how to manage the GST issue with them.

If your customers are households (end-users), the consultant who adds 10 per cent GST to the bill will be 10 per cent more expensive than the competitor who does not charge the 10 per cent.

If you have a part-time job where you are an employee for tax purposes, that income is not added to the income from your own business for purposes of determining whether or not you have passed the $50 000 threshold.

You can register for GST when you apply for your ABN, as shown in Step 5 on page 93.

You have just decided whether you will register for the GST. You have already chosen your business name. You have already decided upon the type of business vehicle you want. It is now time for the next step.

STEP 4: IF YOU ARE GOING TO BE A COMPANY, ACQUIRE IT AND REGISTER IT

If you are going to incorporate and trade as a company, then you can see your accountant, or go to a specialist provider like <http://www.incorporator.com.au> or browse through the *Yellow Pages* and purchase the company yourself from one of the businesses listed under Shelf Company Services. You will need to have answers to the following questions:

- How many directors? You can have sole director companies.
- Who will be the company secretary? It could be you, although many single director companies use their accountant as the secretary.
- Who will be the shareholders? You need only have one.
- What name do you want it to have? Do you have three others in case the preferred name is not available?
- What will be the registered address of your company? This is usually a place which has someone in attendance during business

hours, so many incorporated consultants nominate their accountant's address as the registered address.

- What will be the address at which the business is carried out?

If you are going to trade as a sole trader or as a partnership, you do not have to complete Step 4. Partnership members should, however, draft a partnership agreement with a lawyer's assistance, dealing with the issues listed in Step 1 above.

STEP 5: REGISTRATION OF BUSINESS NAME, ABN AND TAX REGISTRATION

These matters are listed together because you can do them all at once.

(A) REGISTER YOUR BUSINESS NAME

You can register your business name by going to the government Business Entry Point website, which is a link from <http://www.business.gov.au>, and follow the links for registering business names. You can also go to relevant state government departments or business offices in your state. (Their addresses appear in the Resources section.)

The fee for registering a business name varies from state to state, but is generally a little over $100 for three years. Usually the only impediment to registering a business name is its availability.

If you have purchased a shelf company, its original name will most likely have nothing to do with your business. Mine was called something like 137 Honky Tonk Nominees Pty Ltd. The shelf company vendor or your accountant will arrange to have it renamed as you prefer. If you want more than one business name, because you are conducting a number of different businesses, and you want them owned by the company or yourself you can register them in this way at <http://www.business.gov.au>.

If you find that your preferred company name is already registered as a business name in another state, try to register your preferred name with the letters of your state as a suffix to the name. For example, your preferred name is Whiz Bang Freelancing and you are operating in Western Australia, but a sole trader in Queensland has registered Whiz Bang Freelancing in that state. You could try Whiz Bang Freelancing (Aust) P/L or Whiz Bang Freelancing (WA) P/L. It may be a good idea to go down to the ASIC office and discuss the issue in person rather than doing it over the Internet, however.

(B) OBTAIN YOUR ABN (AUSTRALIAN BUSINESS NUMBER)

All businesses need an ABN (Australian Business Number). The easiest way to obtain an ABN is to apply for it on the Internet through the government business website <http://www.business.gov.au>.

You need an ABN to allow you to receive 100 per cent of the moneys you are entitled to under any contract you may enter into. Without an ABN, the hirer is obliged to retain and pay to the Tax Office an amount equal to almost half of the contract value.

Before you apply for the ABN, it is necessary to have chosen your business structure and your business name—that is why this is Step 5(b).

(C) REGISTER OR DO NOT REGISTER FOR GST; REGISTER OR CONFIRM YOUR TAX FILE NUMBER AND FOR PAYG TAX

As you move through the website where you register your business name and obtain your ABN, you have the option of ticking the GST box and registering for the GST or leaving it blank, thereby not registering.

If you are a sole trader you will then be asked for your tax file number (TFN). If you have a new company or partnership, it will be allotted a TFN unless that has already been done by your accountant or the shelf company vendor.

OTHER ESTABLISHMENT ISSUES

The following aspects also need to be dealt with at establishment time, because you will be having business cards, a letterhead and perhaps other marketing materials prepared.

ELECTRONIC ADDRESSES

Website

The website is now the fundamental marketing tool after the business card. Consultants who position themselves as having considerable expertise in a particular field and who work for a wide range of clients, charging higher fees, will be expected to have a website. A website allows prospective clients to see how consultants promote themselves.

The website should show the range of services offered, evidence of previous delivery and how to contact the consultant. It is effectively an electronic brochure, which should be regularly updated. Failure to have a website will indicate that the provider is not at the leading edge, is a little bit out of date and possibly under-invests in their own professional development. Some prospective clients see lack of a website as indicating that a consultant is likely to cut corners by avoiding essential expenditure. For low profiler service delivery, characterised by quasi-employment with few or only one client, a business website is not essential.

If you want a website, you have a number of options. Your Internet service provider will either quote to host your website or direct you to a provider who does. Normal hosting fees in Australia are about $240 per annum, with approximately $120 having to be paid to the domain registration authority every two years. These rates are under pressure to move downwards, however. Much lower rates are available from American hosts, and it is possible to have a free webpage with some email service providers. Free websites might be accompanied by promotional messages which are not symmetric with your services, nor perhaps will they represent 'good citizenry'.

There is abundant software available for constructing a page, including Microsoft FrontPage in the MSOffice suite of programs. Courses are readily available on a local basis. I feel the need to restate the maxim that if you want others to pay you for advice on the basis that the specialist (you) is the source of the best outcome, then you need to engage others, particularly with the website as it is such a public expression of your business and your own standards.

Email address

As discussed in the marketing section (page 138), in the absence of a previous history with a client your address is an important indicator of the quality of your service. While the Hotmail and Yahoo addresses are free, they are an indicator of low investment and a client may have concerns about your capacity to receive documents if you are operating with a free address. I recommend you give full consideration to having a more substantial name behind your business. High profilers need their own domain.

TAX ASPECTS

Your own accountants are the best source of information about what taxes affect you and your plans. There are, however, a few key principles which apply at the date of writing and which may prevail for the next few years in Australia. The results test was described earlier in this chapter (see page 86). Another important principle is the so-called 80/20 rule.

THE 80/20 RULE

Under this rule, any self-employed person who earns more than 80 per cent of their income from one source is not eligible for normal business deductions but is treated by the Tax Office as an employed person. In some industries the government has made an exemption and the relevant industry associations have informed their members of their win in negotiations with the government. For readers of this book, the most likely impact is that those who receive more than 80 per cent of their income from the one client will not be able to gain normal business deductions when they complete their tax returns.

ALIENATION OF PERSONAL SERVICE INCOME LEGISLATION

The main impact of this legislation is that personal service income (consulting, contracting and freelancing) cannot be passed on to non-earners. Other members of the personal service provider's family can only receive income from the family business to the market value of that work. For example, a consultant who earns $90 000 in one year cannot minimise tax by paying $45 000 to their spouse for their services in keeping the business books when those services would normally be provided commercially for $1500.

TAX DEDUCTIBILITY

Many people new to self-employment are not aware of what constitutes a business expense and what is eligible for a tax deduction. As a general rule, if expenditure is for a business purpose, it is a deductible expense for taxation purposes. In simple terms, this means that postage stamps bought to post business letters are a deductible expense whereas stamps bought for family Christmas cards are not deductible. However, stamps bought for business Christmas cards are deductible.

A chair bought for your office is a deductible expense whereas the director's chair for the back verandah is not a business expense. If your business requires that you read the newspaper or a particular magazine that contains articles about the area in which you practise, then the expense is deductible. In summary then, it is the purpose of the expenditure rather than the item purchased which determines eligibility of expenditure as a tax deduction.

SUPERANNUATION

It is a requirement that all employers contribute a percentage of the salary of their employees to the employee's superannuation fund within Australia. If you operate as a company, you are an employee of the company. For some time in Australia, the minimum contribution you need to make is 9 per cent of your earnings.

As sole traders and members of partnerships are not employees, it is not a legal requirement for them to contribute to a superannuation fund. They can make contributions if they wish, but it is not compulsory.

Incorporated consultants who have good years are in a position to maximise the benefits of superannuation as a tax deduction whereas unincorporated consultants generally have less flexibility. The amount of deduction possible under superannuation rules differs according to

the age of the person. It is recommended that you consult your accountant or your financial planner. Providers of superannuation schemes can
also give relevant although not disinterested advice.

Unincorporated service providers may at times find clients hesitant
to engage them due to the number of payments to be processed to pay
the service provider, the Tax Office, workers' compensation authorities
and superannuation funds (see page 82).

WORKERS' COMPENSATION

The rules in each of the Australian states differ in respect to requirements for workers' compensation. This is insurance in the event that an
accident occurs to you in the course of your work. As a general rule,
unincorporated consultants have no workers' compensation and therefore have to make arrangements for their own insurance cover. All other
consultants should make inquiries as to the rules prevailing in the
various states in which they work. A list of the WorkCover offices for
each state appears in the Resources section.

OTHER INSURANCES

In addition to workers' compensation, there are a number of risks you
can seek to manage using an insurance policy.

The first relates to our liability to the general public—public
liability insurance. If in the course of business someone suffers damage,
injury or loss which they can prove is due to our negligence, they may
try to sue us. These types of risks may relate to business visitors coming
to our home offices and tripping over the proverbial bike. A part-time
worker coming to do some typing might suffer loss and damage to their
$3000 notebook computer that they had plugged into our neglected,
unreliable power supply. Some insurance companies offer policies for
small businesses but not all cover home-operated businesses.

It would be wise to check your current insurance policy to ensure
that you have cover for business visitors. It is also important to check
whether you have cover against fire, damage and theft for equipment
such as computers which were previously used for domestic purposes
but now have a business function. Special cover will also be required for

those items you take with you when away from the office, such as your mobile phone and notebook or palmtop computer. Business items are normally covered by an office equipment policy.

Service providers who give advice normally take out professional indemnity (PI) insurance. This is designed to protect them from litigation where their clients consider they have suffered loss and damage through negligence on the part of the adviser. Commonly known as PI, this insurance is often available on the best terms from the professional associations to which the adviser belongs. PI is also offered by major insurance companies and by the Association of Professional Engineers Scientists and Managers of Australia (APESMA), which provides a wide range of services to consultants. APESMA is at <http://www.apesma.org.au>; or telephone 1800 800 998 for the insurance and superannuation services office.

PI insurance is expensive. In some circumstances a client will expressly pay the premium for a consultant to undertake a particular job. To be effective, however, the insurance has to be purchased every year for which the project has life. Consultants who practise on a part-time basis may find the cost of PI insurance prohibitive as it is spread over only a few jobs. There are a number of avenues through which consultants can seek further advice about alternatives to paying for PI insurance.

The first is to seek advice from the insurer as to which aspects of your service delivery are considered the most risky. It may be possible to delete those services or to substantially increase the fees for their delivery.

Some consultants obtain an agreement from their clients that any litigation shall not exceed either the value of the fees paid or the extent of the PI cover. Some insurers, however, may object to such a clause. You would have to ask the insurer and read your policy carefully.

An increasingly common form of protection is for the service provider who is an adviser to have no assets in their own name. After consultation with their lawyers they place their assets either in trust, with their spouse or some other trusted party. Those who transfer all their assets to their spouse are relying on the Family Law Courts to protect them in the event of a breakdown of their marriage. In some situations the non-advising spouse owns 99 per cent of the asset as a joint tenant and the advising spouse 1 per cent as a joint tenant. This is to prevent the transfer of the asset to a third party without both parties signing the transfer. Clearly there are tax implications, and it is advisable to consult your legal and accounting advisers to clarify your own situation. Cases are currently before the courts which may diminish the capacity to remove assets from the adviser's name. Get current professional advice.

Income protection insurance may also be required. The insurer will need to be satisfied that the insured has reasonable prospects of earning the income level that is being insured. Conversley, you need to ensure you are not paying premiums for an income level you cannot prove.

WORKING OUT OF HOME

Local government requirements differ throughout Australia. It is recommended that you make inquiries about the regulations applying where you live. Remember, for most of the businesses we are discussing, clients rarely come to our offices. We generally go to their business address or meet them in quiet coffee shops or plush hotel lobbies, depending on the positioning and degree of acquaintanceship.

The building industry may be an exception to the rule that clients rarely attend our home offices. If you are in this industry you have to pay more attention to the location of your office and the degree and amount of insurance cover you need.

Key points

- Incorporation affords the best form of positioning, particularly for high-profile consultants.
- The sole trader is the simplest business vehicle and the least costly to maintain. However, it may prevent you from working with larger organisations.
- It is easy to incorporate and any service provider can do so if the client requires it for about $550. Otherwise, the larger accounting and consulting firms may be able to provide you with an alternative whereby you work as their agent.
- Choose your business name with a view to its ease of use as a domain name for your business should you later require it.
- All businesses should have an ABN to ensure you can receive full moneys due under your contracts of engagement.
- Only businesses which earn more than $50 000 per annum are required to register for GST.
- It is difficult to claim business expenses as a tax deduction if more than 80 per cent of your income is from one client in the tax period.
- Check on workers' compensation and other insurances as listed for fuller protection.
- Contact your local government authority to see whether any particular regulations affect your home office operation.

6
FINANCIAL ASPECTS

The business conundrum: if I got the job I obviously charged too little; if I didn't get it, it was because I charged too much.

Ian Benjamin

I don't know what I am worth,
I don't know what I can get,
I wonder what I want,
But I am sure of what I need.[1]

Geoff Bellman in *The Consultant's Calling*

HOW MUCH WILL I CHARGE?

Few issues cause more angst for consultants than pricing. While the client is worrying about the problem, the consultant is worrying about what to charge. To lessen the worry and to save you a lot of time, it is a good idea to work out three standard fee rates: premium rate, standard rate and 'mates' rates'. You then apply these in every situation. If the answer is not clear, split the difference.

Let's start by making a distinction between costing and pricing. *Cost* is what it costs the service provider to make the service available.

Price is what you charge the customer. The difference between the cost and the price is your gross profit. To arrive at net profit you need to deduct the cost of your overheads from gross profit. In our business, expenses for each project are normally passed on to the client, and are therefore part of the costing exercise.

In some areas of business, the hourly rates are set and well known to all participants. In many areas where low profilers work, the large hirers dictate what the hourly rate will be. This situation usually sees contractors offering a relatively standardised service, quality is a given, and time constraints are also known to both parties. This leaves price as the major determinant in awarding the assignment to an acceptable contractor.

Higher profile consultants tend to offer a more differentiated service, and so there is great variation in their hourly or daily rates.

SET-UP COSTS

Relax. You probably already own most of the equipment you need. One of the major advantages in operating this form of business is its low set-up cost.

The following table shows approximate set-up costs in Australian dollars for home-based operators operating at different levels of investment and at different levels in the marketplace. Certain assumptions have been made in the compilation of the table. For example, it is assumed that at the medium and higher levels, the consultant's mobile phone would be supplied free under the contract with their carrier. The lower-level operator could make do with a desk from an op-shop or one already about the house. Consultants could consider taking a loan if they had insufficient sums to finance the amount listed in the total row at the foot of the columns.

Set-up costs at different levels of investment

	High $	Medium $	Low $
1. PCs	4 000	2 000	1 300
2. Software	2 000	800	200
3. Printers, copier, fax, scanner	2 200	200	80
4. Laser printer	770	400	
5. Modems/routers	350	200	
6. Mobile telephone	'free'	'free'	110
7. Other			
• Desks	1 300	300	
• Filing cabinets	990	500	110
• Bookshelves	5 000	500	300
• Etceteras	550	300	110
8. Car	c44 000 +	c22 000	c5 500
9. Website	3 000	1 200	300
10. Livery & logos			
• Design	2 200	1 000	
• Letterheads	550	100	50
• Envelopes	300		
• Display folders	1 100	20	20
• Business cards	330	220	66
11. Yourself*	2 200	1 100	880
12. Working capital loan			
13 Legal	1 320	880	
14. Accounting	660	400	110
15. Other			
Total	c\$29k + car	c\$10k + car	c\$4k + car

*Item 11, 'Yourself', refers to what you could spend to improve your physical appearance and capacity to create a better first impression. This may include dental work to give confidence and a better smile. For others it might be the need for a new suit of high-quality fibre, good cut and manufactured with an eye to classic design. Image consultants often recommend their clients adopt an updated hairstyle, possibly for the first time in 30 years!

OPERATING COSTS/OVERHEADS

The overheads are costs you incur by being in business and are generally fixed for a standard level of activity. They are then built in to your standard hourly or daily rate.

The table below shows the overheads for a typical consultant business.

Annual overheads for a typical home-based consultant business

	Medium	Subtotal
Operating services		
Accounting	1 500	
Bookkeeping	1 200	
Legal	500	
Secretarial	500	**3 700**
Office overheads		
Rent, rates, cleaning	—	
Energy costs	300	
Insurances	600	
PI insurance	3 120	
Telephones (1 mobile + 1 landline)	1 500	
Internet/email	700	
Courier	100	
Postal	250	
Post box	55	
Computer requisites	500	
Printing and stationery	300	
Office requisites	700	
Depreciation on equipment (non-cash)	1 500	**9 625**
Superannuation		
@ 9% salary of $60 000	5 400	**5 400**
NB: This is included in hourly rate, as is income tax		
Financial		
Bank fees	360	
Workcare @ 1.2%	720	**1 080**

	Medium	Subtotal
Staff amenities		
Refreshments	550	**550**
Marketing		
Research, design, promotion	2 500	
Webpage hosting and updating	850	
Marketing lunches, coffees	1 500	
Travel & accommodation	1 500	**6 350**
Professional development		
Subscriptions	600	
Newspapers/periodicals	500	
Training & seminars	1 800	**2 900**
Motor vehicles: 3 options*		
(i) Use taxis: 46 weeks @ $100 per week	4 600	**4 600**
or (ii) Acquire a car by personal loan	6 456	***or***
plus depreciation @ 15% (non-cash)	4 500	
plus FBT, say 0.9%	450	**11 400**
or (iii) Acquire a car by lease	6 465	***or***
plus FBT, say 0.9%	450	**6 915**
Plus running costs (fuel, reg., ins.,		
maintenance, parking @ $200)	4 500	**4 500**
Miscellaneous		
Goodwill amortisation (non-cash),		
commissions, other FBT		
ASIC Annual Return	200	
Contingency	1 000	**1 200**
Total expenses	*c*$30 805	**+ car**
		+ salary
	or $29 305	cash (net of
		depreciation)

*You have three options: taxis, borrow + buy, or lease. If you borrow, the loan could be $30 000 at 12 per cent interest with 35 per cent residual in five years. If you already own a car, just include the business proportion of depreciation and running costs.

THE AVERAGE

In talking with many accountants, it appears reasonable to assume that overhead costs on an annual basis for an average business would be in the range of $20 000 to $35 000. For low profilers working as casuals at the clients' premises, overheads may be as low as $7000, plus car plus salary. By way of contrast, a high profiler consultant who has mainly short-term engagements and therefore a relatively high level of marketing expenses, who drives a 'luxury car' and has a commercial office in a business location may have overheads at around the $60 000 per annum level, plus salary.

To see the relevance of overheads to pricing, let's make some assumptions about the average for each type of operator:

- **The low profiler:** Overheads are $7280 per annum or $140 per week. The assumption is that the consultant works primarily as a casual employee for award casual rates, is unable to influence the price at which they offer their services and therefore marketing is primarily of a networking nature involving continual contact with prospects and clients.
- **The medium profiler:** Overheads are $20 000 per annum or $385 per week. The assumption is that this consultant works on medium to long-term contracts for fees that are up to 30 per cent above casual rates. The medium profiler is relatively unable to influence the price at which they offer their services. They have an active marketing function which involves maintenance of a website, networking, and written approaches to prospective and existing clients on a regular basis.
- **The high profiler:** Overheads are $40 000 per annum or $770 per week. The assumption is that this person works on relatively short-term contracts, has some degree of price independence, and has an active marketing function.

For general discussion purposes, let's use the medium profiler rate as the basis for further analysis. This means weekly overheads are $385. To this you can add another $160 per week, that is $8320 a year, to run a car.

This gives us $28 320 as an average annual overhead. Consultants who spend a lot of time working on the clients' premises with tools provided by the client will have much lower overheads.

SALARY

So you need to earn $28 320 to pay for your overheads but you also need to earn your salary. The amount of salary you require will in part be determined by what the market is prepared to pay and in part by how much you actually need. The fee level you set is an indicator of how good you think you are as a provider of your service. Someone who seeks payment at the lower end of the scale is suggesting to the hirer that they perform at the lower end of the scale. Alternatively, someone who asks for a high fee is suggesting that they are confident they will perform well and that they are in a leadership position in the marketplace.

A good way to work out what salary you require is to calculate your annual level of expenditure. If you don't know what this is, work out how much you earned in your last year of employment and then calculate the net addition to your savings from your salary for that period. If your savings decreased, the amount of the decrease would need to be added to the salary earned and spent. The opposite applies if your savings increased during that period.

Maybe your venture into consulting or freelancing is associated with a change in lifestyle. You may be proposing to simplify the way you live and therefore spend less. After considering all these factors you will come up with a desired salary in your first year as a consultant. There is an exercise at the end of this chapter that will help you determine your daily and hourly rates. In this case let us assume that the salary you require is $80 000. This is $1538 per week.

If you are a consultant providing a readily available service like bookkeeping, drafting or engineering maintenance, then it is probable that you'll more or less have to accept what the hirer is offering—working for the 'going market rate'. There will, however, be a range of fees paid and you can use marketing strategies and tactics to position yourself within this range.

PRICING: CONVERTING YOUR SALARY INTO A DAILY RATE

Having decided to pay yourself a salary of $80 000 per annum, you need to calculate the number of weeks in which you can earn fees. Having done that, the next question to answer is how much of each week is billable time. This concept is sometimes referred to as the utilisation rate.

Employees in Australia generally work between 44 and 46 weeks a year: 46 weeks if they keep good health, 44 weeks if they use their two-week sick leave entitlement. In calculating the base fee level, it is worthwhile working through the following procedure.

Forty-four weeks is a conservative starting point as it provides for the full four weeks of annual leave, two weeks of public holidays and two weeks of sick leave. When consultants are new to their businesses, they typically undercharge, tend to take more time to gain client commitment to projects, and are less skilled at managing client postponements and cancellations. To provide for this, a 10 per cent contingency is built in, so that the $80 000 has to be generated over 40 weeks.

In part B of this worked example, you see that after time is allocated to marketing, administration and professional development, there are only three days left in the week for the short-term engagement consultant to earn. For the consultant working on longer term engagements, four days are available to earn fees as it takes one day, on average, to run one's business.

Calculating a daily rate

A: Weeks in a year		52
Less public holidays	11 days = 2 weeks	
Less annual leave	20 days = 4 weeks	
Less sick leave	10 days = 2 weeks	
Equals forty-four (44) weeks		**44**
Less 10% contingency	= 4 weeks	
Equals forty (40) weeks to work		

B: Total working weeks   40

	Time allocation	
Engagements are:	*High profiler*	*Low profiler*
Marketing	25%	10%
Administration	10%	5%
Professional development	5%	5%
Fee earning/billable	60%	80%

C: Proportion of time spent earning fees

Between 60% and 80% (3 days or 4 days per week for 40 weeks)

(If unclear, nominate three days a week billable; if you are a low profiler, choose four days. This will see the high profiler consultant have $40 \times 3 = 120$ billable days pa, and a low profiler $40 \times 4 = 160$ billable days. I think the low profiler consultant should really aim for 180 days. That is, forget about the 10 per cent contingency after the first two years but make sure your fees are adequate.)

Income requirements

	Very high profiler (VHP)	High profiler (HP)	Low profiler (LP)	Our example (MP)
Salary to consultant @	260 000	120 000	30 000	**80 000**
Overheads @	80 000	30 000	10 000	**28 320**
Profit is built into your rate				
D: Total revenue required	**340 000**	**150 000**	**40 000**	**108 320**
E: Weekly rate: D ÷ 40	8 500	3 750	1 000	**2 710**
Short-term engagements				
F: daily rate: E ÷ 3	2 835	1 250	335	**905**
hourly rate: F ÷ 8	355	155	40	**113**
Long-term engagements				
G: daily rate: E ÷ 4	2 125	940	250	**680**
hourly rate: G ÷ 8	265	120	30	**85**

Working through the calculations, you can see that our medium profiler consultant who wants to earn $80 000 per annum gross (inclusive of superannuation) and who has overheads of $28 320 per annum will need to charge between $680 and $905 per day and to be engaged for 120 days at the higher daily rate or 160 days at the lower fee in order to make the targeted income level. (Figures are rounded.)

EXPENSES

Expenses are costs incurred in doing a particular job. The most common expenses are travel, report preparation costs and hiring of other service providers. Expenses are normally agreed to prior to the engagement commencing. The consultant then submits them to the client as part of their invoicing process.

Invoices are normally lodged on a fortnightly or monthly basis. In longer term projects these intervals are usually associated with milestones (identifiable measurable deliverables or outcomes). It is customary to match invoices to the attainment of milestones. It is arguably better for both parties that the invoices are submitted on a regular basis.

Clients generally would rather receive regular smaller invoices that can be seen to relate to particular pieces of work than to receive one very large bill. A client is more likely to appreciate your work and pay your invoice when they know that it is for something they have seen you do recently. From the consultant's point of view, it is also better that the intervals between payment are short to ensure cash flow. Research shows that inadequate cash flow is one of the major causes of failure of small business. Regular invoicing will enable you to provide for normal living expenses as well as covering the expenses incurred on behalf of the client.

COSTING

Cost is what it costs the provider to provide the service. There are three steps in costing a job.

The first is to make sure that you have the brief right. This means that you need to know exactly what you are required to do, what the client expects you to do and what you have agreed to do, by when and at what level of quality. This is the quality aspect of your service delivery.

The second step relates to time. You need to calculate how many days will be required to perform the service. If it is a small job you may have chosen to quote in hours rather than in days. If the job is very urgent and subject to intense time pressure, it is a good idea to quote in hours as you may well find yourself working twelve or sixteen hour days. Once you have calculated the amount of time you will spend on the project, multiply that by your hourly rate to give you the salaried part of your project cost. Many experienced consultants add a contingency to this figure. Quite often projects incur delays for reasons that are beyond your control. If you are inexperienced at costing and quoting on jobs, then it is a good idea to allow for a contingency to cover for overruns.

When a project is very large or goes over a long period of time, a relatively small error of 10 or 15 per cent could have drastic repercussions on income flow. It is a good idea to break large projects up into a number of smaller phases. In this way, when you quote the cost for each phase you are exposed only to a smaller sum.

There are many very experienced consultants who will increase the amount of time allocated for particular projects by a factor of 50 or 100 per cent, or even more, particularly when they are a small part of a larger project. This is because delays are more likely when the scale is larger and when others have control. Experience in this matter will enable you to become more proficient at costing. While you are inexperienced, try to avoid quoting a fixed rate for a project that is of long duration. Endeavour to 'chunkify' your proposal so that you can re-quote for sections of it rather than the full project. This may be difficult if the client, quite reasonably, wants the total project cost up-front.

If your client agrees to pay you on an hourly or daily rate basis, you will not face any risk in respect to time or cost overruns on the project. There may be a problem, however, in estimating when the project is going to finish, which will make it difficult for you to line up subsequent engagements. As a general principle, it is desirable to have the right to come and go on a project, and to have the right to be able to handle more than one project in any period of time. This gives you the flexibility to service more clients and thereby develop a business rather than simply have a substitute job.

The third step is to calculate expenses for the project. This is usually just a matter of identifying the expenses and listing them. You can use phrases like 'accommodation, travel and transfers'. Normally consultants travel and are accommodated at the same level as their clients. In bidding for engagements, you can be more competitive by quoting as a local. You then absorb the travel and accommodation costs yourself. Clients can be grouped so that you spread the fares over a few days engagement instead of just one. You can also use the visit to make valuable marketing calls.

You have now costed this job. Most consultants regularly monitor their level of expenses and their progress on a time basis. If there is divergence from what was planned, discuss it with the client as soon as possible to protect your relationship.

I HAVE THE COST OF THE JOB; WHAT WILL I PRICE IT AT?

There are a host of discretionary factors to consider before you submit your price to the client. You need to consider the particular characteristics of this engagement. If you have a 'pricing policy' then you simply refer to it. Here are the pricing policies typically used by consultants.

SIX PRICING POLICIES

1. Value pricing

(a) What is it worth to the client?
'Value pricing' is very common in consulting. Why did Red Adair, the man who extinguished fires in burning oil wells, charge so much when his work often took only a short time? Obviously the risk was high and there was extensive use of expensive equipment. However, when an oil well is burning off $1 million an hour, the firefighter who can put out

the fire sooner rather than later is in a strong position to ask for a very high fee—it is worth it to the client.

How do you justify the high fee? The answer lies in your expertise. How long did it take you to acquire the knowledge and confidence to be in the position to give advice that can save someone a lot of money, time or other valuable aspect? Years.

You are distilling years of study, experience and reflection into valuable advice. To this weight of argument you can add that you have now taken a risk. You have left your job, invested in a business, spent many hours, lots of dollars and exposed your ego to the tyranny of the market. This client request is your moment in the sun. You can charge them what it is worth to them and they are better off. This is a win-win situation. The fire is out and you are both many dollars better off than you might have been!

(b) 'Solution selling'
By pricing your offer as a 'solution' you are effectively using the value pricing methodology. Estimate what the problem is costing the client and then charge an appropriate amount for your service delivery. Using this approach constantly reminds the client of the value of your work. Solution selling utilises the principles of 'project cost' described below.

(c) The product approach
Many service deliveries can be packaged as products for which a standard fee is charged. For example, where the consultant performs an audit to reveal needs or to meet certain compliance obligations, the fee can be a set price according to the number of sites audited. Similarly, a training program that takes two days to deliver might be charged at $4000 or $6000 rather than sixteen hours' time.

2. Client capacity to pay
(a) Client capacity to pay
You need to consider the positioning of the client in the marketplace. A client positioned at the high end of the market is more likely to accept a higher cost proposal from a consultant. There is an expectation

in the offices of some of Australia's largest companies, for example, that the medium profiler consultants who work for them in the IT field will charge a minimum of $1500 per day.

(b) Charge what the market will bear

Organisations that pursue this variation on 'capacity to pay' usually do so with a reminder that 'we are the best'. They will also stress the benefits to be gained by the client in engaging them. One would need excellent client management skills, the very latest innovations and techniques, and an excellent track record to continually pursue this policy. The 'tangibles' (Chapter 7) will need to be aligned with the fee structure.

3. Market forces: demand and supply

(a) Timing factors

If the matter is urgent, the client will expect that the consultant put all other matters aside and work continuously in the short period of time to resolve the problem or otherwise perform the service. In this instance you are better off charging an hourly rather than a daily rate and your fees can be at the high end of your scale. If you are very busy, you have a reason to quote a higher fee for delivery during that busy time. You may quote a lower fee for a period when you are less busy.

(b) How much do you need this work?

The point above relates to the urgency of the project to the client, now look at it from your own perspective. If you have had a quiet time over a protracted period, or if you are starting up, you may offer your services at a lower price.

If the assignment has particular appeal because it allows you the possibility of enhancing your skill base, industry knowledge or knowledge which can be used to advantage in the future, then you may benefit by lowering your fee.

(c) Market price for this type of work

In the case study on page 118 ('When the lower price was worth it'), the client and I both knew that training providers at their level in the marketplace (tier-one firms) normally expect to pay around $1500 as a minimum for a trainer. If you charge less than this you may be regarded as not being to an appropriate standard.

(d) Competition
This is also a determinant of what price to charge the client. The tendering process is very good at exploiting the competitive aspect of bidding for jobs.

4. Strategic pricing

(a) Future prospects with the client
You may see this opportunity as being the forerunner of a lot of work and so you set the price on a more attractive level to the client compared with what you might otherwise charge at this time and for this type of client.

As a general rule, avoid lowering your fees to a level that makes you unhappy. If you are unhappy it will probably show during the course of your delivery.

History with the client is a relevant factor in price setting. If you do a job for mates' rates when you start your business, the invoice should mention the normal rate for the job, then say on the next line 'but as agreed' with the agreed amount. This will remind the client of the real value of your work.

Many leading firms use this introductory rate approach to win bigger business. Prior to the client organisation undertaking a major project, a big consulting firm will put in key personnel at lower than market rates so that they can be in the box seat to build key relationships and even to influence the scoping of the project. They get to know the client's decision-making personnel, the context in which the services are to be delivered and the way the organisation functions. In this way they effectively write themselves into the brief.

(b) Volume considerations
To pursue the point above, if there is the prospect of high volume work with a client, then a good case can be made for a rate reduction in the

client's favour. This is particularly so if it involves a lot of repetition—such as audits or training programs. If the consultancy is a large and complex assignment, then that is prima facie a case for higher rather than lower fees. See the case study below: 'When the lower price was worth it'.

(c) Risk

If the risk associated with any project is particularly high, the fee should similarly be higher. The consultant's liability will be greater and there may be a need to consult other specialised advisers. This is likely to result in relatively costly professional indemnity insurance premiums, which need to be paid for by the consultant.

(d) Transfer of intellectual property (IP)

If the consultant is transferring intellectual property to the client, the fee will be much higher than for the mere provision of time. An example of this would be a training provider who licenses the client to run the training course itself within their own organisation. The licence will have a fee based on the number of 'users'. Software companies also charge on this basis.

5. The three times multiple

This method suggests the consultant should charge themselves out at three times the hourly rate of an employee. This reflects the common assumption that one-third of the fee is salary, one-third is overheads and expenses and one-third is profit.

In practice, many organisations have sophisticated accounting systems and quite often internal consultants provide services within those organisations at a fee which is approximately 2.5 times the hourly rate the employee consultant earns. Using this methodology, an employee who earns $80 000 per annum will, if they work a 38-hour week, earn $40 per hour. The hourly rate for this employee when they function as an internal consultant who is being charged out in the organisation is either $120 per hour (3× multiple) or $100 per hour (2.5× multiple).

6. Your 'three rates policy'

At the start of this chapter I suggested that we should all have three rate levels: premium, standard and 'mates' rates'. This saves a lot of angst and time wondering about what to charge. If your client is a major publicly listed company, it will expect to pay upwards of $1500 a day for a medium profiler. If the client is a not-for-profit enterprise doing good deeds, then make your own contribution by charging your lower 'mates' rates' amount—if you don't, you are highly unlikely to get the job.

As a guide, my premium rate is 30 per cent higher than my standard rate. The 'mates' rates' are 60 per cent of the standard rate. If you are doing work for charities or some good cause, then you might be better off to donate your time than to work for a 'Mickey Mouse' rate: that is, a very low one.

WHEN THE LOWER PRICE WAS WORTH IT

I was invited to make a submission for the conduct of twenty one-day workshops for 200 lawyers in a tier-one legal firm.

I thought about it and put in a bid at $1650 (which included GST) for one workshop. If the client wanted at least ten of these then my fee would be $1100 each. The month was October and the twenty programs were to be delivered by Christmas. I didn't have twenty days available in the time, and suggested that if they wanted twenty then I could continue through to March.

The training manager responded by inviting me to do a one-day workshop that would be attended by the HR manager and the training manager. They had invited three providers to each run a trial program and would select one to do the other twenty programs.

The day came and I did my presentation with at least one of the managers in the room and ten lawyers. It went well and about three days later I was invited to train all 200 lawyers.

At Christmas I went in to see the training manager (the client) and give her a small Seasons Greetings gift—a bottle of champagne. We were halfway through the twenty groups at this stage and it was proceeding well.

I asked the client, 'Why did you choose me?' She responded with, 'There were three reasons. First, the workshop is very good;

there is a lot of variety and participation. Second, when you did the trial presentation, you did not try to sell yourself or editorialise about the workshop. You let us judge it for ourselves. That was good. Third, and I am afraid this was a consideration Ian, your pricing was very attractive.'

I knew one of the other tenderers. It was a well-known firm whose price would normally be about $3000 per workshop. I was very happy with the engagement. Twenty days' work with one client is about 7 per cent of my annual target. It carried on for three years and then led to an engagement in that firm's offices in another state.

PRICING QUESTIONS

DO I CHARGE A DAILY OR AN HOURLY RATE?

Hourly rates are preferable for rush jobs as in these situations you may be working sixteen or twenty hours a day. On the other hand, the daily rate keeps calculations simple and most consultants work on the basis that they will under-sell and over-deliver. It is quite difficult to do eight hours' work for one client in one day working from your own office. Telephone calls, emails, visits and other clients all compete for your time. Keeping a logbook can be a great help. In most instances, a day is eight hours. Professional associations of practitioners will give clear indications of prevailing work practices in different situations.

CAN I CHARGE FOR TRAVEL TIME?

Do you want to travel from Brighton to Broadmeadows, from Cronulla to Castle Hill, from Broadbeach to Ashgrove, Tuggeranong to Belconnen or from Hamilton to Auckland or Wellington for a 30-minute appointment? Try to have a minimum consultation time, say three hours. This covers travel time. A one-hour appointment may take half a day or longer when travel is included. Alternatively, charge for actual travel time.

At times, however, you may need to catch a flight to another city to secure a consultancy. The cost of this may represent only a 10 per cent deposit on the first engagement!

There is no clear convention on travel time. Big firms tend to claim that they charge it, but it often relates to the relative competitive position in which the supplier and the purchaser find themselves. It is common to hear of half rates for travel time, or for no time charged but a greater gross fee. Clients used to big firm consultants may expect you to charge for travel time. It is normal that the first hour of travel is not charged. After that time, fees, or some other reward, should be contemplated.

PRICING PRINCIPLES
Focus on the project cost
When communicating with your client, it is often helpful to focus on project cost. The emphasis here is on what the project gives the client (meets their need), not on your hourly or daily rate, which could be two to three times the rate paid to a salaried full-time employee. As a general rule, minimise communications about your daily rate and maximise communications about satisfying the client need, solving the problem (providing the solution), getting things fixed.

If your client is one of those organisations that is happy to hire you for an indeterminate period of time, then of course you will be happy to work for the hourly rate providing you have some indication as to when the agreement will end.

Practise rate preservation
This can be summarised as keeping your perceived market rate up, and finessing the hours. Protect your nominal rate, that is, your published hourly rate. If you want more work but the client thinks you are expensive, charge for less time but keep the hourly rate up. This protects your positioning and sets the benchmark for future work.

Up-front fees
These are desirable but often hard to negotiate. They are, however, to be considered in the following situations. Up-front fees are essential if the client is in trouble. Be careful giving advice to clients who are in financial trouble. It is possible that you can be considered to be a director

of a company if you act like a director, even though you have not been appointed as one. Directors of companies that continue to trade when they cannot pay their debts may be personally liable for those debts.

Up-front fees can also be appropriate if the consultant is required to make concessions such as committing to be in a certain place at a certain time, thereby saying 'no' to other clients; incurring costs such as travel expenses or production of a report; or when you find yourself allocating considerable time to a project in the expectation that some subsequent event will yield cash.

Up-front commitment fee

Most of my engagements are between half a day and four days duration. In my proposals I invite client acceptance with the following paragraph:

> Should you wish to accept this offer, please convey your acceptance to (my email address) and pay a deposit of $1,100 (including the professional fee at $1,000 plus $100 GST into our account at (Name of Bank) BSB (x digits) Account # (y digits) in the name of (account name) or mail to the address in the footer of this letter.
>
> A tax invoice can be forwarded to facilitate confirmation and engagement.

This clause works well as it makes clear the next step for the client and I don't deter other potential clients or purchase any airline tickets until the deposit comes in.

Success fees

These are paid to contributors to projects, including consultants, when certain targets are met or surpassed. They are very hard to measure. The contribution by any party tends to be diminished over time, during which circumstances change and others make useful contributions. Try always to invoice and receive payment when the value of your work is more obvious to the client. As a general rule, this is sooner rather than later. Avoid taking 100 per cent of your fee as a success fee. You cannot live on hope! However, a success fee may be the very thing that makes you rich!

Development fees

The client may assume or want ownership of the intellectual property or copyright for a new product you have developed, such as a training program, if you invoice them for its 'development'. This matter should be addressed at the start of the consultancy and referred to in the brief.

Contra

Consultants are often in a position to help one another, as they tend to talk as quasi-colleagues. This could be viewed as friends helping one another. Instances of consultants doing work on a contra basis for a client are less common, as many organisations would regard it as in-appropriate. I have heard of consultants accepting office space for work but such arrangements need to revert back to market values for both parties to be satisfied in the longer term.

Retainers

These are less common in the past decade as clients become more project focused. In business they can be used to keep the experts away from the competition. While the advantage to the consultant is a regular cash flow, the consultant needs to know when they will be required to deliver the services and needs to know this in advance. Retainers can limit your flexibility to be available to other clients and they may also jeopardise your independence.

VARIATIONS

The need to get the brief right in order to allow for optimum service delivery has already been stressed. It is common, however, for the brief to change as the project evolves. This is particularly relevant where the organisation is large and your intervention is relatively minor in its operations, or where the project is long term. Your letter of engagement therefore needs to have provision for variations to be made.

Variations need to be in writing and it is preferable that they have the client's signature of acceptance on them. If you have ever engaged a builder to construct or renovate a house, you'll know that variations tend to be priced on a higher basis than the original tender proposal. It is up to individual consultants whether they choose to adopt this practice or not. Variations may require that you have to renegotiate arrangements with your associates, suppliers and other clients.

RING RING, RING RING

Is that your phone or mine?

'Hi Ian (insert your name). I'm Nick Costello. I manage Radio Station FMzap at Port Macquarie (insert a regional city that is on the coast and four hours' drive from your office). You did a job for my mate Sally Bigelow at FMzap in Brisbane (insert your home town). I want you to come here, mate, and do that training (insert what you do) job that you did for Sally, here at Port Macquarie. I saw you run a one-hour version of the program at the radio industry convention at the Gold Coast last year. I understand it takes you three days to do and I would like you to do exactly what you did for Sal. Okay mate? I've got twenty people working here, she has 32. The only difference is that we have only three people on news and Sal has fifteen. She and I get all the same feed from the national network. How much will it cost, do you reckon?' says Nick.

I say, 'Nick, thanks for the call. I'd be pleased to do it, thank you. Can I have your number and I'll get back to you today? I'm just on my way to a meeting and I need to talk to you about dates, and a couple of other aspects about your business, if that's okay.'

'Sure Ian,' says Nick. 'The number is (02) 6666 6666 and my mobile is 0419 666 666.'

'That's easy. I'll call you after 4. G'bye Nick.'

I hang up.

You now have to work out how much it will cost you to deliver and what you will charge or price it at. We shall return to this later in the chapter. But let's note a few things now.

You will not say a price off the top of your head because you cannot remember what you charged his colleague in your home town. You expect that Nick will know this figure, and while the price will be reasonably consistent for the same service you can recall that you did this earlier job some time ago when you were keen to get business. In more recent deliveries, your rate is probably higher.

Second, you do not know how you will get there. Flying is an option, but you are not too sure about accommodation charges and the cost of car hire. On the other hand, it might be good to do it in the holiday period so you could take your family there and have a few days away.

It may also depend on when you do it; you are very busy in the second and third months from now but you could easily do it in the next few weeks and that includes school holidays.

You the reader can have a think about this for a few pages. Essentially you will need to do three things in costing and then pricing this job. You will need to:

1. Have a standard daily rate that you can quote. This rate will be sufficient to cover your overheads and pay your salary component. This is the labour cost component and will be one of your three rates referred to earlier.
2. Calculate the expenses for the project that you will incur in the delivery. This is the expenses aspect of the cost.
3. By adding 1 and 2 together you have the cost of the job. You now need to consider a range of aspects to give you the price.

By the end of this chapter you will be able to quote a price. Hopefully Nick won't have gone to anyone else!

HOW DO I NEGOTIATE FEES?

Negotiation of fees is a key success factor for anyone in business. If you find yourself doing the job for much less than you consider it to be worth, there is a tendency to be resentful, to procrastinate and perhaps not to do the best possible job. It is therefore just as critical to get the price right as it is to get the brief right. These issues are both addressed at the first stage of any client project. The following six-point process is an excellent guide on how to negotiate your fees.

1. KNOW THE MARKET

If you know the market rate for your type of service and you know where your prospective client sits in the market, then it is unlikely that either party will bring unrealistic expectations to the negotiating table. The consultant who is used to quoting their services to clients located in Governor Phillip Tower, 101 Collins Street or the Riparian (all premium buildings) should not be surprised if there is resistance when they quote the same rates to organisations in the not-for-profit sector.

The principle of the marketing mix is that all the components of the marketing strategy should complement each other. The price therefore needs to be consistent with the quality of the product, the promotional strategies used, your address, the way you present in person, and your track record. Marketing is more effective when it is focused on the market segments that are ready to receive overtures from providers who have arranged their marketing mix to target those segments.

So that you will always have a good idea about what the market level for fees is, keep networking and when you hear about work being done you can ask, 'What sort of money gets paid for that type of work?', or similar vernacular words. Sound casual and unobtrusive.

2. SELL THE BENEFITS

The consultant will win more engagements if they focus on demonstrating to the client the benefits the clients will receive. These will be the cost reductions received, the market advantage gained, the implementation of the difficult aspect of the project for the next quarter, or the feel-good aspect which will occur after the project's delivery.

3. LET THE CLIENT RAISE THE ISSUE OF PRICE

Quite often the issue of price will not be discussed in the first meeting with the prospective client. After that meeting, the consultant will go back to their office and prepare a proposal showing the client how they can have the benefits of the services within the organisation. The price will be just one aspect of this proposal.

It is best not to start the project until the client has agreed to your price—and expenses. If the client does not give you the acceptance in writing, consider sending an email saying, 'I confirm your acceptance by telephone today that I am to go ahead with the *Winter Project* and that the total costs of this project shall be $5000 for professional fees plus travel and accommodation expenses as described in my proposal to you of (date)'.

4. WHERE THERE IS RESISTANCE, ASK 'WHAT DID YOU HAVE IN MIND?'

If there is resistance to your fees, there are two schools of thought as to how this might best be handled. The big firm approach is normally to continue to sell the benefits. If market conditions are tight and they are keenly seeking work, a more accommodating strategy is adopted.

Under these conditions, you ask the client this question: 'What did you have in mind?' This requires the client to raise the issue of price first. When their rate is much lower than what you had in mind, you have a mismatch.

5. A MISMATCH? VARY THE DELIVERABLES

If the suggestion is that your fees are too high, the classic consultant response is to vary the deliverables. This means that you accept the lower fee being offered by the client but will reduce the scale of delivery or gain some other aspect that you desire. This may include secretarial assistance being provided by the client, provision of car parking or agreeing to certain come-and-go preferences of the consultant. The consultant might reduce their daily rate if the number of days for the assignment is increased. This is a normal discount for volume approach.

I reduced the cost of a project by $1000 by having the client purchase my airline ticket from Melbourne to Auckland. They have special arrangements with a multinational travel firm that I could not obtain. Another way of reducing the cost of hiring you where travel is involved is to bracket interstate clients together so that only one airfare need be purchased.

6. CONDUCT A RELATIONSHIP MARKETING PROGRAM

The final aspect of the negotiations is to endeavour to influence the context in which negotiation and service delivery take place. You may partly achieve this by conducting a relationship marketing program whereby the client continually derives some benefit or pleasure from your association. The timing of your negotiations can also be important, particularly when you know the details of the client's objectives for the period and progress to date in achieving them. The main element of such a program is personal contact on a regular basis where you continually invest in the relationship. It is also characterised by the regular provision of information from you that is perceived as valuable by the client.

These six steps are sequential and will lead you to more effective negotiations and better outcomes in your relationships with your clients.

RING RING, RING RING

That's Nick.

I had left a message on his mobile at 4.15, just 30 minutes ago: 'Hi Nick. Thanks for calling back. That price Nick, I have sent it to you by email, and it is . . .'

WHAT WAS YOUR PRICE?

Here are the issues:

1. What was the brief? Same as for Sally here in Brisbane. Except that there are twelve fewer people. Does it still take only three days? If it does take more time, this will need to be included in your quote. Let's assume that there is no extra time and there are twelve fewer manuals to be supplied. You are charging $27.50 including GST for each one.
2. My daily rate is $800 plus $80 GST. This is what I charged Sally and it is still the same rate, so that is $2400 plus 240 GST = $2640.
3. Expenses. Two ways to do this: either quote the fee plus expenses or detail the expenses. I know Sally wanted the expenses listed so I will do the same for Nick.

Here are the items I will need to cover:

(a) Airfare to Port Macquarie or drive car?

Airfare is $550 return. Plus taxis at other end to the hotel, then to their office five times, plus once to the airport on day three. You ring and find out that the office is a $10 taxi fare from the recommended hotel. Airport $30 from hotel. Taxi bill estimated at $110. This is cheaper than a hire car. Can walk to dinner at night. Allow $90 to park my car at airport in Brisbane for four days. Total travel cost by flying is $750. Time used in travelling is about five hours but it is at the end of the day in both directions so I will absorb this item.

or:

To drive my car there and back is 800 kilometres: I can charge the 800 km to them at 60 cents per kilometre, which is the ATO rate for my 2.5 litre car. This totals $480. It will cost me about $160 in petrol plus ten cents per kilometre for running and depreciation which is another $80 plus I have to drive for eight hours. I would charge that at half rate, so total amount I would invoice the client for driving would be $480 plus $440 which is $920.

Decide to fly: less hassle, unless I take the family. Either way I tell the client I will make my own travel arrangements and invoice him at the end of the project for $920, as that leaves the options open and gives some reimbursement to me of about $170 towards travel time if I fly.

(b) The hotel is $99 per night including breakfast. I would want to get there the night before so that I am fresh to do this job. So allow $300 for accommodation.

(c) Meals: allow on a daily basis, $35 for dinner and $10 for lunch, including GST. Breakfast is included in the hotel bill. That totals $135.

(d) The training component requires manuals, which I charge at $27.50, which includes $2.50 GST. There will be 21 of these—twenty participants and one for me. There is also a manual that I leave behind to assist them with the process. It costs $55 including $5 GST. I hand out chocolates that will cost me $20. Total cost of training materials will be $652.50, which includes $59.32 GST.

(e) What about Internet time, phone calls home and glass of wine at the end of the day? I will wear the cost of these. They are tax deductible and I allowed for them in my overheads when I worked out my rates at the start of the year.

The total bill will be $2640 professional fee and $2007.50 expenses. Together they total $4647.50, of which $422.50 is GST.

GETTING THE MONEY IN

Credit managers have a saying that goes: 'There is no such debt as a bad debt, there are only old debts'. Earlier we addressed the issue of the risks involved in working with clients in financial hardship. In such instances it is important to receive payment up front and to invoice regularly at short intervals. Effectively, a COD (cash on delivery) plus seven or fourteen days relationship.

The same principles apply for other clients: regular, smaller invoices which you follow up by telephone if the account is overdue. It is normal commercial practice in Australia to pay accounts somewhere between 30 and 60 days. Many businesses have shorter intervals but they usually have control over one of the key inputs of your production process, like your telephone or your power supply.

I am aware of one instance where an engineering consultant was owed $45 000 by a client. The original contract provided for payment upon completion and the work was to take place over six months. After four months, the client went into receivership and subsequently liquidation. The consultant was an unsecured creditor and received nothing.

As in marketing, the most effective methods of gaining a client response are the ones that involve you personally. Telephoning, visiting, and remaining persistent yet pleasant will most likely see you collect moneys owed to you without undue delay. A common reason for late payment is incorrect invoicing.

Sample invoice

FINBAR CONSULTING PTY LTD
ABN 95 003 373 208
Box 1001
Parramatta NSW 2124

30 June 2007

TAX INVOICE

INVOICE TO:
Ms Meredith del Porto
General Manager
Circle Line Manufacturing
1011 High Street
BOTANY NSW 2019

Attention: Meredith del Porto

Tax Invoice #: 2007/064   Your Order No: 987665/0KUP
Our ABN: 95 003 373 208   Your Order Date: 4 June 2007

We hereby present our account for the services as follows:

Date of service	14 June 2007			
Service	Report on 'Compliance Readiness' for Circle Line Manufacturing, Botany Storage Centre at 14 June 2007 according to ISO 9000 specifications in 4 colour, triplicate hard quality and CD ROM as agreed			
Conducted by	Gerald Finbar			
		Fee/cost	**GST**	**Sub-total**
Fee		$2500.00	$250.00	$2750.00
Expenses	Secretarial	$300.00	$30.00	$330.00
	Paper & Binding, CD	$247.75	$24.78	$272.53
	Sub-total	$3047.75	$304.78	
Total				**$3352.53**

Thank you for the opportunity to provide our services.

Yours sincerely

Gerald Finbar

Terms: 14 days please
E & OE

2007 AUSTRALIAN CONSULTANT MARKET MODAL RATES

Market	Client type	Fee range per day	Comment
Helping fields	Not for profit/ education/ community health	$250–$500 $1250 (government policy work)	Government will pay more in these areas for policy work
Management consulting: specialist projects	Government departments: e.g. Tourism, ATSIC, Defence	$700–$800>> $1200–$1500 for more senior consultants	Longer term sees lower rates than shorter term
Engineering & training	Industry	$800–$2500	
IT	Big business/ government	$1200–$2500	High profilers can be paid much more
General consulting	Universities & TAFEs	$800–$1200	'Celebrity professors' get much more
Management consulting & training	Banking finance, big corporations	$1500–$3000	
Management consulting	Big firms	$800 for a junior to $4000 for a senior partner	Juniors are new graduates. Senior partners may charge up to $650 per hour
Management consulting	Medium firms	$800 for a junior to $3000 for a senior partner	
Key-note speakers	Fee levels in various markets are reflected in fees paid	Full day fee for a 1-hour presentation $1200–$5000	A lot of preparation is required. 'Stars' can receive much more
Contractors	Any field	Approx. 125–150% of the equivalent FTE rate	FTE: Full-time employee

EXERCISE: HOW TO CALCULATE YOUR DAILY RATE

This exercise will show you how to set your daily rate. Choose the level of overheads that will apply to your business, the salary you need and the additional amount you would like. There is an example worked through in the right-hand column.

1. Your requirements PA $000

		Example
(a) Overheads @ $7.5k, $10k, $15k, $20k, $25k = _____		$20
(b) After tax income (minimum) = _____ (i.e. what you must earn to pay your bills to live)		$40
(c) 20% of (b) for tax = _____		$8
(d) Other income I want (gross: inc tax) = _____ (i.e. what you want in addition to (b) and (c) as just reward for your efforts and the risk you take. In this example, the person wants gross income of $70k as that is what they used to earn)		$22
(e) Total = $ _____k pa		$90k pa

2. Working 40 weeks in the year:

$e $\dfrac{\_\_\_\_\_}{40}$ = _____ (y = income required per week)

e.g. $90k/40 = $2k p wk

For high profilers

y ÷ 3 = $\dfrac{\_\_\_\_\_}{3}$ = $ _____ daily rate

e.g. $2.25k /3 = $750 p day

For low profilers

y ÷ 4 = $\dfrac{\_\_\_\_\_}{4}$ = $ _____ daily rate

e.g. $2.25k/4 = $563 p day

3. Acid test $\dfrac{1a + 1b + 1c}{40}$ = $ _____ per week for survival

e.g. $52.5k/40 = $1312 p wk
$328 p day

Notes

1. Recommend that low profilers divide the total income (e) by 44 instead of 40 as they should really target more than 160 days pa (try 180–200; but may be only 160 in year one).

2. The 20 per cent for tax is an average rate, not the marginal rate.

3. In this example I have nominated $20k as the overheads. Low profilers and some medium profilers might just keep them to this level, particularly if they work from home and have low transport costs. Contractors should be able to keep them low as they may be 'quasi-employees' with long-term engagements.

4. On anecdotal evidence, I would say that incomes of independent consultants reveal a bi-modal distribution. I hear many stories and some evidence of net incomes in excess of $150k pa and many at $50k pa.

Key points

- Cost is what it costs you to provide the service. It includes your notional salary. Price is what you charge the client.
- The price for any service delivery is a combination of your fee for the time involved, the expenses you incur and a discretionary adjustment that will depend on a range of factors related to urgency, expectations, risk, use of intellectual property and the intrinsic value of the work to the client.
- Your hourly or daily fee comprises a component for your time and a component for your overheads. Overheads are the costs you incur irrespective of the amount of business you do in the short run. Overheads do not vary in the short term, but they do in the long run.
- You need to establish a notional salary, your hourly and daily rates.
- The same job may be charged at different rates to different clients.
- Have three rates—premium, standard and 'mates' rates'. The same job may be charged at different rates to different clients.
- Low profilers tend to be price takers, that is, they take the fee offered by their clients. High profilers have more discretion in setting their own fees.
- Travel time is negotiable depending upon the relative importance of the project to the client and to the consultant.
- Do not quote a price until you know how much it will cost you.
- Always let the client raise the issue of price first, but do not start the job until it is agreed.
- Request a deposit as confirmation of your engagement.
- Issue invoices promptly, and for regular smaller amounts. Follow up when they are not paid, first by sending a reminder, then by telephone.
- Stay up to date with market rates by constantly asking questions of clients and providers.

7
MARKETING YOUR BUSINESS

The old adage says: 'It's not what you know, it's who you know.' From my experience, 'It's not who you know, it's who knows you!'

You have two options when it comes to marketing your business. One is to get out there and market yourself. The other is to stay home and wait for the phone to ring. If you choose the latter, you can usually do so without any interruption at all!

MARKETING: THE FIRST STEP

1. UNDERSTAND WHAT IT IS

Marketing is all those events that lead you to be in direct contact with the prospect or client. It is about attracting interest in what you have to offer. To get prospects interested in the first place, you need to be positioned where they will see you and in such a way that they will become curious about what you have to offer.

You will also need to know your service or your product, and to know yourself. Arguably, you are 'full bottle' on both!

2. KNOW HOW MARKETING DIFFERS FROM SELLING

Marketing occurs first and is completed once you have their interest and attention. Then selling occurs which is 'enabling the transaction' or benignly 'convincing the prospect to purchase'.

Often the best way to sell is to talk to the prospects—about what they do in their businesses—and then to relate success stories (experiences) about what you have done in working with others in their situation. This is what interests them. They will start to ask questions—and then the marketing is completed. You then go on to secure the engagement—place, time, task to be addressed—and ascertain what they will give you in return. More of this in the next chapter.

Marketing is one step in the process of doing business. If the business process starts with the vision of the entrepreneur, the identification and confirmation of values and the determination of goals, market research is the next step.

3. DETERMINE IF THERE IS A DEMAND FOR YOUR SERVICE

Few consultants do formal market research. Most consultants have extensive market knowledge about their area and use that as their basis for planning. They know other providers and often model their own business on what they can see others doing. It is also usually the case that they are aware of two or three potential clients who would engage them now if they were available.

One of the best forms of research a new consultant can undertake is to go and speak to people in the industry that you propose to service. Ask them how things are going, what the issues are and what they see as needs to be satisfied by providers to that industry. Senior industry participants may even become your advocate if they are impressed with your ideas and your ability to articulate your plans.

There are a number of organisations that can help you with information about the market. In some states you should contact the Business Enterprise Centre, in others the Department of Small Business. Outside the capital cities the regional centres often have extensive advisory services. See the Resources section for information on services available in your region.

STEP 2: ADOPT 'BEST PRACTICE' TANGIBLES

Taking this step will see you avoid one of the biggest pitfalls of independent consulting and small business generally. There are seven vital matters to attend to before you start marketing so that you can do so with a degree of confidence: an essential ingredient of successful marketing and selling. These are known as the 'tangibles'—aspects of your service delivery that the client can see, hear or experience in some sensory dimension. The most important tangible is yourself.

Cheap tangibles are the most obvious indicator of a poorly prepared business and a disincentive for clients to engage you. Cheap tangibles suggest the consultant cuts corners, is unwilling to invest in quality outcomes and is unprofessional.

Service is a part of all business transactions, and in consulting the 'service component' is 100 per cent of your offering. Service is an intangible item. Its value is not proven until it is delivered. So in order to form a view as to how good the consultant (or any business) is, clients look at the tangibles.

While references from previous clients are valuable indicators of quality, any prospective client will need a certain degree of comfort before bothering to inquire about the nature and extent of your relevant track record. This comfort will need to come from the tangibles: how will the prospective client come to the decision that it is worth pursuing an investigation of you as their preferred service provider?

So what are these tangibles, these clues for the prospect about the reliability of your service? Apart from the testimonials, that is.

1. YOU

We need to look like, speak like, listen like and relate like we are professionals who are keen and competent to help others in their businesses.

Some useful sayings give good messages here to help us present as a 'quality tangible':

- 'You have one chance to make a good first impression.'
- 'Your attitude is the most important aspect of your appearance.'
- 'Dress how you want to be perceived.'

Books are written on each of these themes. Fashion and style are for you to decide, but I have some recommendations about quality and cut. Synthetic garments can look shiny and cheap and be smelly in hot weather. Cottons, wools and leather have a textured appeal and can usually avoid these problems. As to cut, classic designs tend to look smart for a long time.

As a coach to many consultants and senior people in professional firms I have often been thanked subsequently for advice to cease wearing short sleeves. A third point is that clothes designed for the beach and night clubs are probably inappropriate in most businesses.

Language is another domain where an approach that is too casual can diminish your appeal to clients. My advice is to avoid swearing, use of words that some find blasphemous, baby talk ('ta') and lazy diction.

2. YOUR ADDRESSES

Your letterhead bears your business address and your electronic address. As discussed in Chapter 4, both are concrete tangibles with strong positioning associations. If the address has adverse positioning consequences, then it may be worthwhile to use a post office box address located in a business precinct. The practice of listing a post office box as your business address is quite acceptable for most consultants. Some use their accountant's office as their mailing address and as the address on their letterhead. Alternatively, there are businesses that specialise in offering these services. Some of them use premium buildings in the city and the address is often on the top floor of those buildings. To use such an address as an independent businessperson seems to me to be tantamount to telling them that you work from home! You may well give out the very message you are trying to hide.

While a post office box may appear insubstantial, you can compensate by over-investing in your other tangibles. This could include having a second colour on your letterhead and business card, having your own Internet domain and having a quality profile document that you can leave with interested clients as a marketing tool.

Free Internet addresses may be fine for personal use but your clients could view this as cutting corners and under-investing in your own business. Clients may also have concerns about the confidentiality of their communications with you and about your capacity to deal electronically with substantial documents.

3. PRINTED MATERIALS

Spend a few extra dollars to improve the quality and range of your hard copy materials, including your business card and website. If you have additional tools such as brochures (a printed page from your website will do at start-up phase) and documentary evidence of your service delivery (reports, manuals), make sure they look and feel good. Find a good designer to produce your livery or 'look'. Offer some prizes to the local teacher of graphic design so students can produce a logo that you must own.

Print business cards in small numbers at first as you may change or add key information early in your consulting career. Once you start crossing out parts of the card it is time for a new one.

Letterheads which you generate yourself, marketing letters and final reports look better when they are printed on higher quality paper (90 gsm or heavier). The cheaper 80 gsm paper readily available in post offices, supermarkets and stationery stores is more appropriate for working documents and internal use.

4. PROMOTIONAL MEDIA

The media you choose to promote your services will also help position your business in the minds of the target market. While a handwritten note pinned on a noticeboard in a ferry terminal can be a very effective method of selling a second-hand bicycle, it is unlikely to win you an engagement as a copywriter. The time and expense incurred in placing notices on noticeboards or advertisements in newspapers could be better spent in attending a publishing industry early morning breakfast and networking with those who have come to hear an interesting speaker. Better still, of course, if the speaker is you!

5. YOUR FEES

What you choose to charge communicates very effectively to the market how much you think you are worth. It also indicates in broad terms the quality of your service delivery relative to that of your competitors. It is more effective not to publish fees until you have commenced serious dialogue with a prospective client.

6. YOUR ASSOCIATES

That kind person who made the referral (of your name) to a prospective client in the first place can be considered an associate. Their reputation and positioning will be another tangible indication of the quality of your service delivery. We are judged by the company we keep!

Your client list and organisations who promote you are further indicators of your service quality.

7. TESTIMONIALS

You will need to refer prospective clients to a third party who can verify your claims of competence and capacity to deliver. If you don't have this third party, then your claims are unsupported. A previous employer or colleague can be the referee or testimonial provider when you start out. It is a good idea to do one or two jobs early for 'friendly parties' at mates' rates. These become the launching pad for future work as they are the first entries in your track record as a consultant.

Testimonials need to be authentic so take note of what clients say when they express approval. I am often told that my work is very practical. When I started, I had some testimonials from unnamed parties which read:

> The following comments are often made about Ian's work:
> 'Practical, content rich, ideas you can use straight away', and
> 'Ian is an engaging presenter'.

While these statements did not have an individual's name to them, I promised to provide referees to interested parties. I still use that method for obtaining third-party recommendation to corroborate the claims made or implied in my promotional material. As you develop your business, your client list and organisations who promote you are further indicators of your service quality.

8. TELEPHONE ANSWERING

I have left one of the most important tangibles to last. From the client's viewpoint, their first experience of you may be a telephone conversation. Here the tangibles would be, in sequence: how the phone was answered, your telephone manner (polite, businesslike, friendly, helpful or otherwise), your voice (pitch, modulation, accent, clarity) and how well you listened and responded to what the caller was saying.

A prospective client calling on a business matter would expect that the telephone would be answered in a businesslike manner. I recently researched how a range of professional firms answered their telephones and from the results recommend the following three-part telephone technique:

a. **Greeting** 'Good afternoon'—this allows the caller to tune into your voice. The caller can organise their approach to the male/female, accented/non-accented, older/younger, senior/junior voice which answers the phone. The greeting may also be spoken over beeps if the call is a long-distance one.
b. **Confirmation** 'Celebrity Photography'—this is the announcement of the business name, giving confirmation to the caller that they have the right number.
c. **Ownership** 'This is Luisa Johnson'—this is where Luisa gives comfort to the caller that someone at Celebrity Photography is prepared to take responsibility for the conversation about to take place. Luisa uses her surname as she wants to differentiate herself from junior staff who typically answer only on a first-name basis.

Imagine what the caller thinks if the phone is answered in the same way as a home telephone. They may well think that they have called the wrong number. Similarly, children, dishwashers, vacuum cleaners, dogs, cats and televisions are all inappropriate background noise when conducting business conversations on the telephone.

The same applies with the message-taking capacity on your voicemail. Messages that apologise for not being able to take the call waste time and are a statement of incapacity.

Consider the alternative responses below. Which message is positive?

This is Damien Watson. I'm sorry I'm unable to take your call right now, but if you leave your name and number I will get back to you . . .
or:
This is Damien Watson. Thanks for calling. Please leave your name and number and I will get back to you . . .

Notice that the first message opens with an apology, tells the caller what they cannot do and in fact wastes time as the caller already knows that Damien cannot take the call because his message facility is functioning.

Mobiles which invite the caller to press a button to leave a number make it difficult for the client to do business with you. If the client cannot leave a number they may well go on to the next service provider on their list.

A final word on the tangibles can go to Oscar Wilde, who is reported to have said, 'Only a fool doesn't judge by appearances'. This is something to bear in mind as you seek to influence your positioning and your prospects of engagement.

STEP 3: PREPARE YOUR SIX-PART MARKETING MIX

This is the marketing plan—a component of your business plan. In this you work out how to present yourself to the marketplace: what services to offer, at what fee level and how you will promote your business. Developing high-quality tangibles will see you significantly along this path already.

You will need to determine your primary promotional tools: a website, any printed materials and whether you will advertise, and so on. You will also need to think about what addresses and phone numbers to put on your letterhead and business card. Will you have a separate telephone number? Will you approach the market with a suit or a more casual look? You have already decided if you will work from home or from a commercial office. These are all marketing issues and together they make up your marketing mix.

The marketing mix needs to be designed to attract the prospect to you, the service provider. It has six components that are complementary and need to reinforce each other. As there is a saying in marketing that 'your worst piece of marketing positions you', these components need to be of a consistent quality. Failure to address this is often responsible for new consultancies not succeeding.

The first four components of the marketing mix are product, price, promotion and place. These are often called the Four Ps of marketing. Let's consider them from the perspective of the independent consultant.

1. PRODUCT

Product is the services you offer. Sometimes you may also package up some of your services carrying a certain price tag. An example of this would be a training program, an audit or some form of compliance assessment. As you are in the service business, product also includes yourself as the service is inseparable from the service provider. It is essential to 'productise' some of your services to add a tangible dimension to what you offer. If all you are selling is your time, that will not be an attractive offer to potential clients.

2. PRICE

Price is your fee schedule. This aspect of the marketing mix sends a strong message to your prospective clients as to where you see yourself situated in the marketplace. It is also indicative of the quality of your service. As a general rule, do not publicise your fees but be prepared to disclose a range when asked and to put a definite price on jobs that you quote. Always quote the range in relation to a deliverable as it focuses on what the client receives rather than what they pay.

Make it your policy to give the client different priced options; you don't always know their budget.

3. PROMOTION

Promotion refers to the means by which you send messages into the marketplace. The most significant of these for a consultant is your own networking. By going to where the clients and other market participants are, you come into contact with people bearing opportunities. Another effective form of promotion includes speaking at seminars and workshops, and participating in the professional development activities of organisations. Creating publicity in the media raises your profile, is free and is usually indicative of having some credibility. Other forms of promotion include having a website, promotional literature including brochures, advertising, and any form of exhibition or demonstration.

There is a great range of techniques and tools you can use to promote your business. As a maxim: When engaged, exceed expectations. Which of the following strategies can you effectively employ to market the services of your business?

The promotional activities listed here are sorted according to the level of personal interaction required and the extent to which they are an event that you plan and organise, or a behaviour that you continually adopt.

Active planned promotional strategies

These are planned events that you organise or someone else has organised and in which you participate.

1. Personal marketing: formal networking. Target key people in key organisations.
2. Cultivating circles of influence. Perhaps other suppliers to your target market—parallel professionals.
3. Speaking externally at seminars, conferences, etc.
4. Running seminars internally for clients. Build your credibility.

5. Having lunch with clients or inviting them to a dinner with a special purpose, e.g. speech, launch.
6. Entertaining: in a very modest way (suggest going to an event together when you have a spare ticket).
7. Engaging a public relations consultant. They may be able to get you exposure.
8. Creating publicity for reporting in the media. Works well in regional areas.
9. Exhibiting: sometimes it is more effective to leverage off the events that others create. Ask questions of existing exhibitors rather than creating your own exhibition.
10. Launch/events. Good for when you start.
11. Requesting mentorship from someone you respect. They may well become your advocate.
12. Conducting a survey and publishing the results.

Many of these active deliberate strategies are forms of personal marketing. This is you being out and about networking, going to functions and seeing people. It is best to think of these activities as personal live marketing. Such marketing is more effective when targeted. It is not enough just to be going to events: it is far more effective when their purpose is aligned with your own. Arguably this is the most effective form of marketing. It is interactive, it is true to life and, on some occasions, you have no competition.

There are a number of personal marketing activities in the next bracket as well.

Active promotional behaviours

These are attitudes and behaviours that you adopt and exhibit.

13. Personal marketing: socialising, having coffee.
14. Telephoning (or emailing) people—just to stay in touch and to pass on information that they may find useful. Emailing is less active as it is not face to face. Email works well if the client has a preference for it and it is a good supplementary activity to phoning.
15. Being seen in the marketplace.

16. Telling success stories. This involves casually relating information about successes achieved which usually involve your input, or the methodologies that you practise, being successful.

Passive promotional strategies
These are tangible items that you create and use.

17. Acquire quality tangibles. You will be assessed on what people see and hear.
18. Newsletters: can be hard work but are an effective way of staying in touch providing you write about what your market is interested in rather than about yourself.
19. Website: essential for high profilers and very good for everyone else. It is a form of marketing support but if interactive can be designed to generate business as well. Once someone has heard of you or met you, they are likely to make a check of what you do if you have chosen to represent it on your website.
20. Direct mail: useful when starting up your business or when you want to give it a boost. Relatively expensive because you need to have a quality marketing tool such as a flyer, brochure or PDF file produced. There will be high wastage as response rates are likely to be low (0.5–2 per cent), but it is better than waiting for the phone to ring.
21. Strategically advertise: in the journals that your prospects and clients read and respect. Advertise your products and have an offer for respondents.
22. Publish. The easiest way to do this is to have articles printed in organisations' newsletters.
23. Email. Good for promoting events and products. Email can be okay for continuing contact with target market but lacks some intimacy.
24. Send useful information by email or in the post, showing off your expertise and helping your client.
25. Sponsor some activity or event in your target market.
26. Leverage off partnerships: creating synergy in this way is cost effective and can enhance your capacity to deliver because there are now two or five of you instead of just one.

27. Leverage off advocates/sponsors.
28. Leverage off professional associations and industry bodies by speaking, training and writing.
29. When engaged, exceed expectations!

4. PLACE

There are two meanings for place, as far as consultants are concerned.

The purist definition refers to the distribution channels for the delivery of your services. In most cases distribution will be live—you will be face to face with your clients. Some may have online delivery over the Internet.

The other aspect of place is your address of business. Chapter 4 has considerable detail on the appropriateness of post office boxes, Internet addresses and whether or not to have a website. It is important that your address conforms to your clients' expectations of your quality of delivery.

For service businesses it is valuable to treat these final two components as separate mix items.

5. PEOPLE

People, to some extent, has already been covered under product. It includes your appearance, attitude and body language, as well as your experience and qualifications. It is more about how you relate to your clients.

6. PROCESS

This is what people experience when they endeavour to do business with you. If a prospect contacts your business when you are not there, what do they experience? Best practice would be a diversion to your mobile phone, which you either answer personally or have your voicemail cut in with a succinct, positive message.

Clients have different preferences and may place more emphasis on one part of the marketing mix. Some are more responsive to a particular form of promotion, others give greater weighting to price, and some look for service aspects or product features which meet their individual needs. It is useful to undertake some research to find out about these preferences.

YOUR MARKETING MIX POSITIONS YOU

Your positioning in the marketplace is largely determined by the way these six Ps of the marketing mix are assembled. Positioning occurs all the time. It is the continual evaluation of where the business sits on a number of planes. The positioning as perceived by the client will to a large extent determine whether or not the service provider will be engaged.

Positioning can be determined in relation to any of the following:

* competition
* quality
* range or type of services
* price
* availability
* access to post-service assistance
* any part or sub-part of the marketing mix.

What follows are the high and low points of positioning for an independent consultant. Read these and determine where you want to be.

Product

High: consultant has breadth and depth in service niche. Has some deliverables that are priced for delivery as distinct from an hourly or daily rate.

Low: consultant has general description of service offerings; can only provide a daily or hourly rate as terms of engagement.

Price

High: $2000 a day plus.
Low: less than $700 a day.

Promotion

High: consultant has website, flyers as descriptors of service offerings, is featured by other organisations as speaker or writer and when Googled brings up five or more references.

Low: no Google recognition, no tangible materials other than business card and letterhead, no leveraging through other organisations.

Place
High: own domain, commercial business address.
Low: no domain, residential address.

People
High: smart and industry appropriate.
Low: not readily identifiable as a person in business.

Process
High: responsive, positive, clear, professional.
Low: phone is answered as 'Hello', not answered in business name.

To get the best possible view of how you are seen in the marketplace, it would be useful to have your clients and other interested and knowledgeable parties complete a positioning exercise as well as doing it yourself. There is a sample positioning matrix for downloading on my website. As positioning takes place constantly, it is a good idea to regularly review your marketing mix and update it in accordance with changes in client preferences, market trends, the extent of your services, and the currency of your promotional tools, including your website. The other Ps of the marketing mix should also be included in this review.

STEP 4: CREATE YOUR MARKETING TOOLS

Packaging your services into products makes your offer more tangible and reduces the personal aspect of the transactions which may be uncomfortably high for many consultants. These products are your standard services written up with limits and prices. When you customise them, they become services. A training program, an audit or a needs analysis are examples of 'productised' services.

Products have the following attributes. They:

- meet a specific need
- take a certain amount of time to acquire/deliver
- have a price or range of prices

- contain intellectual property or something else of value
- provide defined benefits
- have a name
- are specific and can be readily described in writing.

The last attribute means that a one-page description of your services can be readily produced for a client. You can have a number of them in a folder to take on your marketing visits. You may post some on your website.

WHY DO I NEED PRODUCTS?

It is much easier to sell a product than it is for a consultant or freelancer to sell themselves on an hourly rate basis. Clients find it easier to make the purchase decision about these things than they do to engage someone for an indefinite number of hours on a seemingly very high hourly rate. This is because the hourly rate may be viewed as too high and the benefit as too vague or speculative.

While products are easier to sell, their primary function on the marketing side of your business is to attract the attention of the client. Once the client is interested, ask probing questions to find out what their particular situation is and what their needs are. They will probably say that they are interested in part of your product, and then they will want to explain what is going on in their business or organisation and how that 'product' might help.

Products are so vital for your success that we need to consider the case for them in greater detail.

You need products for market entry

- Products develop your profile. Profile is what people know about you. Being heard, read and seen will help people learn more about you and products will result in that happening. To a minor extent at least, you become a sort of celebrity in your field through the leverage provided by products.
- Products enable people to see what you do. The one-page flyer depicting the product gives the client a good understanding of the

benefits you can bring to their organisation. It gets you in the door. You then put the product aside while you ask them what they are focusing on in their business.

- Products give you something to sell, something other than your time which always sounds overpriced and sometimes vague as to the benefits you can deliver.
- Often products are sold for a relatively low price and so the authorisation to engage you can be made at a lower management level than the decision to hire you for a couple of months, even though the initial engagement may lead to a longer term engagement after your first service delivery. The client may like to trial you for a very short period by purchasing the small product and after being very satisfied with your first performance will have the confidence to book you for a longer period. If you consider the list of products below you can see that many of them would be delivered in the earlier stages of a project.
- Once you have made the first delivery, the client is likely to ask 'What else do you do?' The products make that discussion simple.

Other good reasons for products

- Developing products is a good investment for future profitability. Your better products will be continuously in demand by clients. Continual modification will be necessary but the initial time spent in development will bear dividends.
- Developing products will reaveal to you the strengths and weaknesses of your service delivery. You will readily identify what you need to do in the way of your own professional development.
- No longer will you be 'between engagements'—that ineffectual euphemism that's meant to conceal that you have no engagements. If you follow this model and become a regular deliverer of products, you will always have something on, even if it is only doing a free talk for a service club for 15 minutes. Once you get on that circuit, there will be no stopping you, providing you deliver value in your talks.

Here is a list of three types of products that service providers can package as services with all those attributes listed above:

Diagnostic products

- Audits, needs analyses, stakeholder surveys and/or gap analysis
- Feasibility studies, market surveys
- Measurement, evaluation, certification.

Writing products

- Manuals, articles, specifications, plans, proposals, briefs, reports.

Facilitation products

- Facilitate: meetings, planning sessions, conferences, debriefings, problem solving
- Transfer skills (train)
- Coach
- Speaking: deliver talks, conduct briefing sessions
- Expert witness
- Broker (be a go-between)
- Manage project.

HOW DO I MAKE A PRODUCT?

There are seven steps in making a product:

1. Identify the need the product addresses.
2. List and describe the benefits of the product.
3. List the deliverables—what the purchaser actually receives.
4. Describe what happens when it is delivered.
5. Develop the content and process you follow when delivering, in detail.
6. Give it a name.
7. Price it, promote it and choose the distribution channels for delivery.

Steps 1 to 6 above are the 'P' product of the marketing mix. The seventh step is the other three 'p's'.

VIGNETTES

In Chapter 2 you saw how to produce a vignette—one of the most effective yet easy-to-produce passive marketing tools. It is a mini case study highlighting part of your experience, a cameo of your own work experience that illustrates what you can do. There are two vignettes in Chapter 2. Here is an additional one for Susan, who became an environmental consultant after working in local government as a planning officer.

ENVIRONMENTAL CONSULTANT VIGNETTE

Situation The suburban council where I worked was considering re-zoning urban bushland for the development of sporting arenas and other community infrastructure.

Challenge I had to ascertain the attitudes of existing residents, community groups and business people to the proposed development.

Action I established information booths in the three nearest shopping centres, arranged for council staff to be trained in interview techniques and then scheduled and conducted regular information sessions over a three-month period. I then rigorously collated the findings and presented the report to the project manager and to the relevant council subcommittee. I also prepared press releases and briefed the mayor, councillors and the CEO on the issue.

Highlights The project became so well known in local government circles that it was used as the model for future development and other community issues in our council. I also delivered a paper at a conference for local government officials.

Ideally, you will develop many of these vignettes demonstrating what you have done and can do. Make them more elaborate with logos and photographs so that they take up an A4 page, or you may make them simple with two or three to a page. For maximum effect, make sure that they are grouped so that you can present yourself as having specialist skills as opposed to being just another person looking for a job.

The headings in our example above are a change from the earlier prescribed STAR pattern. Using *Challenge* instead of *Task* and *Highlights* instead of *Results* is arguably superior positioning. We consultants overcome challenges rather than just perform menial tasks!

THE MINIMUM CONSULTANT MARKETING TOOL KIT

FOR THE LOW PROFILER

1. **Business cards** Competently designed, lots of space, showing your name, the business name, mobile number, electronic and business postal address.
2. **Letterhead** Either printed on 90+ gsm paper or in your computer for you to create your own letterhead. Most communication is electronic.
3. **Profile document or flyer** One page on A4 paper, showing your range of services and contact details.
4. **Vignettes** Illustrating the type of work you have done, either as an employee or in your own business. These can be part of your profile document or separately attached to marketing proposals.
5. **Testimonials** From previous clients as you develop your business.

FOR THE HIGH PROFILER

1. **Business cards** Lots of space, professionally designed showing your name, the business name, mobile number and website. Ideally it will also show your dedicated landline, fax number, electronic address and place of business and postal address.
2. **Letterhead** Printed on 90+ gsm paper or in your computer for you to create your own letterhead. With compliments slips—three to an A4 page.
3. **Profile document or capability statement** From three to five pages, showing your range of services, contact details which should be on every page in the footer, statement of track record (best if this is in mini case study/vignette format), your methodology (how you work), names of previous clients (providing there is no breach of

confidentiality), testimonials and awards, and details of how to take the next step towards engaging you. It may also have vignettes attached. If the nature of your work enables photographs, then these should be included, and perhaps one of you.

4. **Testimonials** Or some form of third-party endorsement from previous clients as you develop your business. The statement 'Referees can be provided upon request' is a minimum offer on your part.

5. **Vignettes** Illustrating the type of work you have done in your working life, either as an employee or in your own business. These can be part of your profile document or separately attached to marketing proposals.

6. **Product flyers** A4 pages containing descriptions of your products.

7. **Website** This can contain the information which appears in your profile document, your products, some vignettes, and articles either featuring you or that you have written. The website should be inter-active, enabling clients to register their interest so that you can contact them. This is called a 'response mechanism'.

8. **Samples of your work** Reports, training manuals, reviews or other tangible evidence of what you do and how you are rated.

OPTIONAL MARKETING TOOLS IN ORDER OF EFFECTIVENESS

1. **Articles** that you collect, or have written, can be sent to interested parties as appropriate. If you send someone else's article always reveal the source and write a summary or synopsis in the accom-panying email to show the client that your referral is considered and that you respect their time. Post your own articles on your website or blog but beware of spending too much time blogging when you could be out networking in person.

2. **Newsletter** produced by you and containing items of interest to the readers that will enhance your reputation as a specialist and source of useful ideas and information. Given that you need to make contact with your client base and prospects ideally on a quarterly basis, the newsletter is a very efficient way of managing this objective.

3. **Emails** which are 'catch-up' notes or you may make referrals to websites that your prospects may find interesting.

Marketing tools of negligible utility include CDs and PowerPoint presentations. Their main weakness is that they are impersonal. Postcards, sent at start-up time, can announce that you are now in business and can also give a brief but interesting description of some of your products or services. Cards and small gifts along with greeting cards, if you know they will be appreciated, can be appropriate.

STEP 5: NOW, DO SOME MARKETING!

Completion of Step 3 above gave you your marketing plan and Step 4 the tools to use while implementing it. You are ready to go! Here are some more ideas. You really do need to be happy to get out and about making personal contact—networking.

NETWORKING

The most effective marketing strategies have you as the main event. Personal networking, where you email, telephone and visit prospects and members of your network, is what will lead to engagements. The purpose of the networking is to stay in touch and find out what others are doing. Demonstrate an interest in them and what they are doing, rather than going about telling them what you are doing. That will come out in the course of conversation.

Have coffee, breakfast and lunch. Go to seminars and invite prospects and network members to go with you. Become a person who is a fount of ideas and who is committed to making things happen. Be patient and take comfort from the fact that you have quality tangibles. Know that any visit to your website by a prospect will stimulate ideas of how they may use you to help them achieve their corporate objectives.

Most consultants get most of their business through word of mouth. It follows that networking will normally be your most important marketing strategy. I started this chapter with the old adage, 'It's not what you know, it's who you know', and commented that in my experience in consulting 'It's not who you know, it's who knows you!'

A final word about networking. It has three major benefits:

- The environment in which networking takes place is a personal one or one with strong personal overtones. It is conducive to building relationships and ultimately receiving referrals. In this respect, it boosts the number of engagements of professional services in the same way that hot weather boosts the sale of cool drinks.
- Second, it has been demonstrated repeatedly by professional firms that networking is what brings in repeat business and new business.
- Third, it is the least costly form of marketing.

CASE STUDY: NETWORKING WITH COFFEE

A small group of consultants in south-east Queensland wanted to build up their client base in the area of providing workplace health and safety services. They had very limited funds for marketing purposes. Once a month they invited prospective clients, including human resources managers and workplace health and safety officers, to afternoon tea at their Brisbane office. The office was in a commercial district, a little tired but very clean and tidy.

In sharing tea, coffee and biscuits with their guests they asked them what their experiences were in the matter of rehabilitation. They found they had much in common. Their hospitality was often repaid with visits back to the sites of their guests. In this way the relationship developed and the consultants built up a list of prospective clients with names, occupations, employers, addresses and even details on their interests and experiences.

The next step involved inviting the guests back for a special talk titled: 'What to expect in workplace health and safety if there is a change in government at next month's election'. Two months later they put on another talk: 'Ten questions about current audit practices'.

The hospitality and persistence was rewarded when one of the largest supermarket groups in Australia gave all their consultancy business in north-east New South Wales and south-east Queensland to the group. The consultants continued the process for three years with considerable success. It was discontinued as the composition of the group changed, as it was seen to have fulfilled its original purpose and that there was now a need to adopt a fresh marketing approach.

PASSIVE 'DIRECT MAIL' MARKETING

Here is a very effective strategy to develop a new service or give your bookings a boost. It is based on the work of American HR consultant Geoff Bellman and I have adapted it and used it to great effect at various times. Others have enthused about it as it gives coverage, is passive (low on personal contact in its early phases) and is effective.

It has six phases:

1. Identify a group of prospects that will be interested in one of your services. A few years ago I did this with tier-one legal firms. I selected six firms and included on the target list the following people: anyone I knew in any of the firms, the managing partner, director HR, learning and development manager, and partners in the sections that I thought had a greater need for the training I offered (it was a course in presentation skills).

2. I wrote four articles and two newsletters that featured articles on speaking in public. I had plenty of material as it all came from concepts in my courses. Examples of this appear on my website. All my newsletters contain tips on how to consult effectively. You should be able to write with similar confidence in your area of specialisation.

3. Surface mail is used to send the first article and a very short cover letter personally addressed by me in blue ink from my fountain pen. I then emailed three days later to inquire as to whether they had received the article. In most instances I did not get a response but that was OK. The articles were in colour and interesting.

4. A month later I sent the second article—electronically but not as an attachment. Then one month after that, being the third month of the cycle, I sent a newsletter which contained another article on presentations as well as other interesting material. Then the same process continued, although in this second cycle I used 60-day intervals.

5. At the end of the process I emailed the addressees offering to meet to discuss how they could develop the effectiveness of their public-speaking commitments.

6. I telephoned those who responded to my emails and arranged meetings where we discussed their situation.

The results? I had some meetings, and within the first year two of the firms engaged me to deliver presentations skills training. In the next year, a third firm engaged me. Within five years I had extended the coverage to five firms of the orginal six. At the same time I was using an additional strategy—leveraging off professional associations by running my workshops for a prestigious organisation within the market and giving short talks at many other venues.

Sending useful information to prospects, customers and clients is another way of building profile and of 'putting in'. This information may be some of your own work, or may be ideas and comments from specialists in other places that you have gathered in the course of your own professional development and research.

SPEAKING AND WRITING AS PROMOTIONAL ACTIVITIES

One of the major purposes of the marketing program is to let market participants know that you are available for hire, so it follows that any activities which get your message to large numbers of prospective clients effectively and on a low-cost basis are well worthwhile pursuing. Two means of doing this are speaking and writing.

Much speaking and writing about business takes place inside industry organisations and professional bodies. Such entities draw their membership from people who want to stay up to date with what's happening in their industry or in their chosen area of service provision or occupation. Each of the entities is in a competitive position, with other organisations appealing to the same membership base. A perennial problem for the people who run these organisations is the need to find people who have something credible, new and useful to contribute and who can present it in an engaging and interesting way.

Association general managers have a double need for talented speakers and writers, as they use them not only to maintain membership levels but also to raise attendances at and revenue from the events they hold and to increase sales of the publications they produce. Hence society executives are always willing to hear from someone who is able to credibly present themselves as a specialist, who has something new to say or write, and who can do so in an interesting manner.

From your point of view, as the consultant who is speaking at a breakfast seminar, at a whole-day workshop, at a substantial conference or writing in the industry newsletter you will receive three major benefits:

1. **Exposure** Those who attend the event and those who heard about it will become aware of your specialisation in the relevant field. You will have gained exposure to your market segment.
2. **Credibility** You will have the imprimatur of the organisation, which is effectively an endorsement as a quality professional service provider.
3. **Fee income** In many instances such presentations receive a fee. If not, they provide a marketing outcome that may otherwise have cost thousands of dollars to achieve. As a general rule, presentations that run for up to two hours are rewarded with a pen or a bottle of wine, those of three hours or more receive a fee. In the middle is room for negotiation and indeed the whole process is subject to negotiation.

Different industries follow different precedents, but in all situations you can successfully gain leverage through speaking. In all towns and suburbs across Australia there is an active network of service clubs, every one of them looking for a speaker for about twenty minutes every week. Writing affords you the same benefits, but it is not as personal as delivery through the spoken word. And let's not stop there—you really need to be seen, as well as being heard and read.

CASE STUDY: SPEAKING AND LAUNCH

Jennifer, a Chinese Australian specialist in cross-cultural services between China and Australia, wanted to start up her business in that area. She approached a Chinese restaurateur and a Chinese Australian active in politics to assist her in launching her business into the Sydney business world. They invited representatives from 60 of the largest corporations, professional firms and government bodies in Sydney to attend a pre-dinner cocktail party in the Chinese restaurant where Jennifer would deliver a short presentation on 'Doing business in China? How to meet, greet and eat with Chinese people'.

About 45 people attended the function, held on a Tuesday evening from 5.30 to 7 pm. Light refreshments, tea and alcoholic beverages were served and Jennifer and her two colleagues networked the room, helping to create a friendly and lively atmosphere. 'And what's your interest in China?' was the standard one-liner.

Jennifer spoke for twenty minutes on cultural aspects of Westerners relating to people from the People's Republic of China. She spoke about greetings, ranks, formal and informal protocol, and dining etiquette. She pointed out what the Chinese found difficult or even offensive behaviours and she told the assembled business and government people what the Chinese liked.

Within two weeks, Jennifer had been engaged to do a similar presentation to one of the larger corporations in Sydney and she was also assigned the job of liaison manager to assist a Chinese delegation travelling within Australia in the next month. Jennifer has now grown her business and has a staff of six consultants assisting her to meet the demand for the service.

CASE STUDY: PUBLICITY IN A SMALL COMMUNITY

Anna moved from Sydney to a small community in the hills behind Byron Bay. She is a practitioner of a special kind of yoga. She did the standard start-up marketing activities for people in her line of business. Anna set times for classes, then posted one-page flyers in the restaurants in Byron and in the cafés and halls of the hinterland.

Anna made a point of meeting the editor of the local newspaper and elaborating on the benefits and distinctiveness of the school of yoga that she practised. The editor was quite taken with her story and so she was featured in a half-page spread with photographs and an article describing the form of yoga and its special features. This in turn led to a regular fortnightly session on a community FM station and articles in alternative newspapers and in the newsletters of many of the villages in the hinterland. Anna was delighted. Her business literally boomed compared with the tough time she had had in the city.

CASE STUDY: FRIDAY DRINKS

The following marketing strategy worked very well for a Melbourne consultant when he wanted to start his business specialising in services to local governments.

Simon, a 35-year-old university tutor specialising in local government, had just finished his Masters thesis on competitive tendering when the Victorian government introduced laws requiring that half of local government expenditure would need to be on outsourced services. This effectively created a huge demand for knowledge about the tendering process.

Simon decided to hold regular drinks at his apartment in South Yarra every second Friday, from 3.30 to 5.30 pm. Each fortnight he invited the CEO, HR manager and the manager responsible for the tendering process from his local council to his apartment to meet with their counterparts from two other councils. This meant there were ten people at each gathering, providing they all attended or sent a representative.

As incentives to bolster attendance he offered refreshments, a short presentation on the competitive tendering process, the chance to network and a free copy of his 'book', being his thesis, to all attendees.

Simon approached over twenty councils, so he was committed to run seven of these Friday drinks sessions in the next three months. The demand for his services was so strong that he had difficulty being available to host all the sessions. Simon privately called the process his 'Friday drinks strategy' but it was marketed as 'Briefings in Competitive Tendering'.

CASE STUDY: TELEPHONING

I abhor telemarketing. It really irks me as I consider it invasive and disruptive. However, I know quite a few consultants have used it to successfully start their businesses and therefore I have to relate one of these cases. This technique owes as much to persistence as anything else.

Jane and Paul, freelance photographers in Brisbane, started their business by telephoning over 150 potential clients. Their target list of potential clients (warm suspects) included newspapers, magazines, in-house publication units of major corporations and government departments, advertising agencies, marketing firms, major stores and clothing manufacturers.

They called the businesses at quieter times of the day to ascertain the name of the person responsible for publishing. This was to ensure that the telephone receptionist had time to provide the most accurate information. On another day they would ring and confidently ask to be put through to that person.

Having been connected to the decision-maker prospect, they asked a series of questions about their needs, including the extent to which they used photographers, what qualities or aspects they considered essential in good photographers and what problems they had encountered in the past.

Finally, Paul and Jane asked if the prospects would be interested in a new service that essentially mirrored what the prospects had said they liked. Undertakings were given that the service delivery would be guaranteed, in that if there were any dissatisfaction on the part of the client, no fee would be charged.

While most parties were not particularly interested in a new service, their calls were opportune with two major corporations which had recently been let down by the same photographer, someone with an excellent reputation but who had extended his overseas business interests to the detriment of his local market.

A combination of proficiency and enthusiasm enabled Jane and Paul to exceed the expectations of their new clients. They went on to use this track record to win the confidence of other new clients and to build the base for their successful business.

CASE STUDY: USING SEMINARS

Neil is a Brisbane-based specialist in the writing of business plans. Once a month he would invite representatives of one of the banks into his office in Spring Hill at about 3.30 pm for a one-hour demonstration of the business plans that he wrote for SMEs (small and medium enterprises).

At each session there would be up to five bank managers or area managers who often required their clients to have business plans. Neil showed them his business planning process and pointed out that his plans matched the format required by the bank. He did this for each of the banks. Neil has been doing this continuously for about six years.

The sessions are just like training workshops: participatory, instructive and celebrated with a cup of tea or coffee and biscuits at the end. Neil has been in business for more than ten years and has enjoyed a regular flow of business from the banks. He keeps in touch with the bankers by sending an occasional newsletter or reference to a matter of interest such as an interesting article, a new piece of government legislation or an encouraging success story. This is usually an account of someone who has received a plan from Neil and gone on to enjoy considerable success.

CASE STUDY: AND LET'S NOT OVERLOOK THIS ONE . . .

Chris is a maintenance contractor based in the Hunter Valley of New South Wales. Martin is a public relations consultant in Sydney. Jenny is a freelance musician in Perth.

They have all used the same strategy. Each had one or two clients in mind before they started their business. On starting up they went to the prospective clients and offered their services. The offers were accepted. They all say they did very good work. They then sat back, waited for the phone to ring, and then did more good work. All three have been very successful.

I know many others who have used this strategy. However, when Chris and Martin are engaged, it is normally for projects of considerable size. Jenny, on the other hand, might only have a two-hour gig. As a person who does mainly speaking and training, I have the same dilemma. When the nature of your work is essentially short term, it does mean that you need a large number of clients in any year and that rarely happens without some prompting on your part.

PS: Blogging

Consultants are using blogs to demonstrate their expertise and this may help them win business should a potential client view their blog. Bloggers report that blogs take a lot of time and are less effective than newsletters at creating inquiry. Blogs are also open to anyone to view, including competitors. The interactive aspect is good for making connections. Let's see how they develop.

Key points

- Pay attention to the tangibles of your business.
- Prepare the basic marketing tool kit.
- Prepare short summaries of your track record (vignettes) so that clients can see what you have done and what you might do for them.
- Create product packages so that clients will find it easier to engage you.
- Use the products to attract clients. Once you are face to face, start asking questions. Be a consultant, not a product flogger!
- Use the marketing power of organisations and networks to promote your name.
- Do your own marketing audit: Are you conveying a consistent message with your six Ps marketing mix?
- Refrain from putting out any substandard marketing materials.
- Be proactive. Try some of the activities listed in this chapter. If you stay home and wait for the phone to ring, you can probably do so without any interruptions at all!

8

SECURING THE ENGAGEMENT

Start with where people are before you try to take them to where
you want them to go.

Jim Rohn[1]

Your marketing program is underway. You have let your contacts know
that you are in business and have given them your details and a list of
the services and products you offer.

Soon you expect someone to contact you in response to your
marketing activity.

When you meet or talk with the prospect, you will need to establish
some form of rapport, a degree of comfort so that the prospect will feel
confident in discussing their business with you. Then you need to
undertake some form of diagnosis to find out if there is a need that you
can satisfy.

When the need is identified, the prospect needs to be convinced
that it is worthwhile addressing it. Finally, you will need to be able to
convince the prospect that you are the person who should be trusted
to do the job. What you will be doing is commonly called selling.

WHY IS IT NECESSARY TO SELL?

There is a need to sell. Selling at its most benign level is simply taking the order. At its more active level, selling is convincing the prospect to make the purchase. I like to think of it as facilitating the engagement—an enabling activity.

Selling is making it easier for the client to engage you. If you leave it up to the client to make the approach and to initiate the engagement, it is highly unlikely that you will have much success. There are many reasons why it is going to be up to you rather than the client to take the initiative to have you work for them.

First, the client may not be aware that they have a need for your service. You think they have the need because you specialise in an activity which is used to help the client, but the client has far more things to think about than the small aspect that you service. (I am sure that there are some additional software skills that I could benefit from learning; however, the need has not yet been demonstrated to me.)

Second, the timing of the approach is often inappropriate. The prospect may be aware of the need but has more pressing matters warranting their attention.

Another reason to follow up your proposals is that your offer may have some minor limitation on what the prospect needs. Often, rather than approach you to see if you can provide that minor aspect, they will wait until someone comes along with exactly what they want.

There are many instances when your competition will get the business. Their service may not be as good as yours, but that may not be apparent in the eyes of the prospect. Perhaps the timing of their approach was better from the prospect's perspective.

Prospects may have other reasons for preferring your competitor. One common area where this occurs is in marketing to large corporate clients and major government departments. In many instances such clients will only engage 'big firm' consultants as they have a secondary need other than the stated need. The stated need might be 'to improve efficiency' but the real need is to have the imprimatur of the big firm giving a 'tick' to the chosen strategy of the business. By having big firm endorsement, the management team or CEO has the ultimate defence if things go wrong—they were following the advice of the recognised experts, the big firm.

THINKING ABOUT HOW TO HANDLE THE FIRST CONTACT WITH A PROSPECT?

I once attended a workshop conducted by David Maister, one of the world's leading advisers on the professional service firm.[2] He has written extensively and for six years was a professor at the Harvard Business School. Maister's daily rate for consulting is around US$20 000; the seminar cost each attendee A$1100.

On this occasion Maister was speaking to professional service advisers about leadership, and about how to gain the trust of clients. On several occasions during the day he made the point that the best book about business development was written over 50 years ago. By Dale Carnegie, it is called *How to Win Friends and Influence People*.[3] One of the main points in this book is that the best way to influence people is to take an interest in them. Ask them questions, listen and make them feel important.

With this in mind you can approach your prospects.

Let's contemplate the possible mindsets of the prospects. If their approach to you is on the basis of a referral from someone they respect and trust, then you are in a very good position. On the other hand, the following set of views is often articulated about consultants:

- 'Consultants' are expensive.
- I had better be careful with this consultant because if I'm not I will end up spending a lot of money for very little value.
- This consultant could be a wanker!

This is a risk you need to manage. The risk is that, in spite of the good referral or having seen your name in their industry magazine, the prospect may be looking for a reason not to do business with you.

THE FIRST CONTACT

Back to your situation. Reasonably soon, you anticipate, a prospect will respond to your marketing stimuli and you will be talking with them on the phone.

Here is a test: what will be the objective of your conversation?

(a) to secure an engagement;
(b) to secure an interview;
(c) to tell them what you can do;
(d) all of the above.

The answer is (b). (There may be an exception when the prospect is in a faraway place or where the service delivery is relatively small and inexpensive.) When the interview is secured, that person will have an interest in what you provide. They will want to discuss their situation with you. You will be live with the prospect, and a different range of skills will be required to secure you the engagement.

RING RING, RING RING

That's your telephone, Jenny.

'Good afternoon, Stanton Graphics, this is Jenny Stanton.'

'Hello Jenny. This is Rick Cometti. I'm with Performance Computers at Burwood. Your name was given to me by Chris Jenkin at City Peripherals.'

'Hello Rick, how are you?' (*You speak with enthusiasm and warmth to maintain a positive momentum and to give off good vibes!*)

'Jenny, I hear from Chris that you have good ideas and experience in working with computer people so I thought I would get in touch. We've just redone all our marketing and before we set out to tell the world about ourselves, we want to investigate getting all new livery, new logo, new webpage. The lot in fact. Do you get involved with that sort of work?'

This is a moment of truth! Which of these three is the best response?

Response #1 'Not a lot actually. I want to because I have just started my business and that is what I want to do. I have done some courses in graphic design and I have always had that sort of flair.'

Response #2 'Yes. I have done work for Chris at City Peripherals and for a number of other firms in your industry. I could bring some samples to show you if you would like. I could also give you the names of people I have worked for if you would like.'

Response #3 'Yes. I have done work for Chris at City Peripherals and for a number of other firms in your industry. I could bring some samples to show you if you would like. Tell me Rick, how big is your firm at Burwood?'

The answer? Response #3 is best.

Response #1 has three problems. It does not give the caller any confidence that the designer can do the job. The first words uttered are 'Not a lot', meaning 'No'. Finally, the consultant is talking about herself and not the client situation.

Response #2 is better but does not take the lead like Response #3 does. It is appropriate for a graphic designer to take samples of their work to an interview. There is no need at this early stage, however, to offer the names of referees. It is better to focus on the client need. Referees can be offered if and when the client asks for these.

The positive telephone conversation between Rick the prospect and Jenny the consultant should continue with Jenny getting more information about the prospective client so that she will know what to highlight in her interview and what to take with her. She will also be starting to formulate her solution, her designs for the client, in the event that she is successful in getting the engagement.

Finally Jenny will say, 'Rick, I think there would be merit in us meeting and perhaps for me to see you at your business in Burwood. If it's okay with you, I could visit later this week.'

If the conversation had not been a positive one, Rick would be unlikely to invite Jenny to Burwood. If that were the case, Jenny would need to reflect on how she had handled the conversation and what she could do next time. As a graphic designer Jenny should have a standard set of questions that she asks when interviewing prospective clients. It is the same for all consultants, whatever their field.

IDEAS FOR A BETTER INTERVIEW

Prior to attending the interview, check your notes about the prospective client. Have a look at their website and then at the list of questions that you normally ask a client. Think about any other aspect that is relevant to be covered by your questions.

Plan to arrive in plenty of time to park your car. Check that your appearance is OK—look in a mirror and at your feet. Go into the reception area and read what is displayed there. This helps you to focus your mind on the issues that the client sees before them every day.

If you are invited into the client's office rather than an impersonal conference room, take note of how the office is set up. If there are family photos and other personal paraphernalia, be prepared to open a dialogue about personal issues, such as whether you have had a good day or how easy it was to find their offices. If the desk is bare and the room highly ordered, then be ready to get into a discussion about business immediately.[4]

In this interview it is very important that the client does most of the talking. This is so you can diagnose most accurately what their real need is and the scope of the situation. Be ready to answer questions like, 'Tell me about yourself'. Have succinct answers ready and make sure that you do not go on for too long. Be prepared to quote some relevant examples of your work.

You need some standard questions for the client. Here are the ones that I usually use as a basis:

QUESTIONS TO ASK IN THE FIRST FEW MINUTES
1. **How's business?**
2. **What's going well?** It is good when preparatory research reveals some item of current interest to the prospective client. Then you can

comment on this and show that you are familiar with their company and up to date on corporate events. This question also gives the client the opportunity to feel good while relating something that they have recently achieved that you may not know about.

3. **What's new in your industry/market?**
4. **What are you focusing on in the immediate future?** Or you can substitute words such as 'few months', 'next period', 'your current plan' or whatever the client uses to describe their strategic direction or business plan. I try to avoid asking, 'What are the problems you address?', instead asking 'What are you focusing on?' This is because some people become unduly defensive if you suggest they have problems.
5. Really listen and develop the conversation about the matters they raise.

As the interview continues take notes and make sure you have enough information to be able to put an attractive proposal to the client. If the project you are discussing is complex and will extend over several months, then you will have more meetings, meet the relevant people from the client's organisation and perhaps visit a number of sites. If the task is a shorter one, of limited complexity, it may be appropriate for you to send a proposal to the client after this first meeting.

Make sure you ask lots of questions. Paraphrase some of the client's comments—this shows that you are listening and can also demonstrate that you have an understanding of the matter. The interview will also give you the opportunity to quote your other work in saying how you handled a similar situation and giving some details of your experiences, always relating them back to the client's situation so that they are seen to be relevant to their need. It does not matter if you are new as a consultant—you can refer to projects you worked on as an employee. The client's concern is about your skill level rather than where you worked in 2006.

There is a list of additional questions you can ask clients on my website. Follow the links from the book.

RELEVANT EXPERIENCE

For example, Jenny on her visit to Burwood might say:

'Your situation sounds very similar to one I worked on over the other side of town recently. In that instance a business about the same size as yours had broken away from a national franchise organisation and wanted their own branding, with new livery for their promotional materials, including business card and letter-head. They also wanted a new website, new window design, new signs on their delivery vans and new packaging on the boxes they used for packing their hardware.

'I spent a few hours with them building up an understanding of the business, the image it wanted to project, who its customers were and quite a lot of other relevant information. In working with them I came up with a new look and it was just the sort of solution they were looking for—modern but discernible, reliable and comforting, clean and elegant but not too pricey.

'I used my network to have their window and vans badged and I worked with them on creating the website. I can show you some of the materials we developed.

'There! Is that anything like the sort of thing you're looking for?'

Such an approach will show the client first that you understand their position, second that you have worked in this situation before, and third that you have the capacity to deliver an outcome of real value.

Most people in business tend to allow up to an hour for a meeting. Look for clues that the allotted time has expired when you are talking. The client may glance at their watch, or accept interruptions from their colleagues. As you are effectively managing the interview, when you have the information you need you may then say, 'Well Rick, this has been very useful to me, thank you. How about I go back to my office and think about this and then give you a proposal as to how you could use this here at Performance Computers?'

The client will usually say, 'Yes. That would be very good, thank you.' This is said as they are getting up out of their chair and you move towards the door together. It may be appropriate at this stage to ask if you can speak to two or three other people in the organisation, just to get the context right, and to make sure the proposal really addresses the needs of the organisation.

It's always advisable to talk to some of the other people in the organisation affected by your work. These would be the target group, the end-users and other stakeholders.

THE EASIEST SALE

Sometimes you receive a call from a prospect inviting you to attend a meeting to discuss their business. The pivot of the conversation is not what you do and can do, it is about their business and how you may be able to help it perform or improve.

The prospect then says, 'I'd like you to run that program of yours in-house with us. I'll pass you on to Alex, who will make arrangements for the dates and the payment. Give me a call when you've done it and we'll see what else needs to be done then. Good luck with it.'

Such ease of selling is more likely to happen when you have previously worked with that client. This is simply a re-order, agreeing to be at a certain place at a certain time to deliver a certain service. You quite probably do this fairly regularly as the client in your own life. You do it when you purchase the services of a doctor, a vet, an accountant or a lawnmowing person. The original sale was made when you chose the particular service provider over the others available. You will probably stick with them until they fail to perform in some way. Any one of them may be unavailable when you need them, your pet may die at the vet's, or the problem they address is not resolved to your satisfaction.

In all these instances the service provider who has you as a client has a relationship management function to perform. The better this is handled, the more likely you will be to remain as their client, even when problems occur with service delivery. To some extent, therefore, there is a need for continuous relationship management. Essentially, this is ensuring that their needs are met on a personal basis as well as on the technical or professional aspects of your service.

The diagram on the following pages shows the normal process

whereby consultants win their engagements. For complex assignments, stage 2 may involve a number of visits by you.

Client contact process to win an engagement

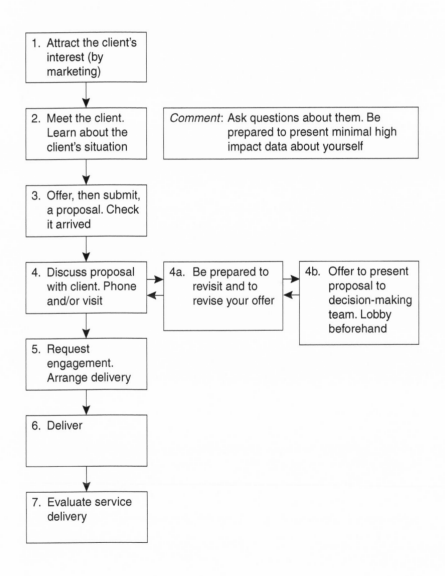

HOW DO I MAKE MY EXPERIENCE APPEAR RELEVANT?

The process of creating interest in your service is usually done by relating the benefits of the service to the client's situation. Research shows that it is more convincing if you create the visual picture for the client of what the situation will be once you have delivered the service. The benefits are what the client gains. Many inexperienced service providers confuse features with benefits. Features are attributes that describe your service while the benefits are the effects of having the service delivered.

For example, a workplace health and safety consultant may describe their service delivery in this way: 'Paul Turner, licensed WH&S Accreditation Officer, based in Albury with twenty years of relevant experience'. The licence, the appellation, the Albury base and the twenty years' experience are all features. In this case, the probable benefits are:

- The work will be done very well (licensed) so that it need only be done once, thereby saving money and time.
- The results will stand up in the event of inspection by a regulator so that the client knows they will comply and avoid fines, thereby saving more money and time. The client will also avoid being named as a non-complying enterprise, which would probably have some adverse effects on their business.
- The Albury base means that for local clients, the cost should be lower, saving both time and money as there will be nil or negligible travel expenses.
- Twenty years' experience should mean that delivery will be quick and expert, again saving time and money. However, some might think that twenty years suggests the service provider is a little too old and may be slow and not up to date. It would be better to say 'extensively experienced'.
- Finally, with all the money and time that is saved, it is probable that the client will enjoy higher profits than if the service is not utilised.

These benefits need to come out in the proposal that you write and in the meetings you have with the client, either in person or on the phone.

WRITING THE PROPOSAL

Chapter 9 includes a draft proposal for a longer term engagement. Here is a draft one for a one-day presentation.

SHORTER TERM SAMPLE PROPOSAL
16 May 2007

Ms Joan Watson
General Manager
Tasmanian Small Business Conference
Level 6, 101 Salamanca Place
Hobart Tasmania 7000

Dear Ms Watson
Proposal for conference: Community Banks
Thank you for the invitation to submit this proposal to participate in your conference in Hobart on 21–23 November. Please consider the information presented and call to discuss any aspect.

1. Introduction
The Tasmanian Small Business Conference is now in its tenth year and the theme is the integration of business with the community.

I have extensive experience in preparing communities in both urban and rural locations to establish their own community banks.

2. Service
To prepare and present two half-day workshops on the theme of Community Banking.

The first workshop will show participants how to assess whether their community has the necessary preconditions to establish a viable community bank.

The second will show how to create the momentum for the establishment of such a bank and how to prepare a proposal to put to the various sponsors of community banks so that the prospects for acceptance are maximised.

3. Timing
At the 2007 conference on either 21, 22 or 23 November.

4. Objectives
To inform the participants about Community Banking so that they can consider whether they will apply the techniques they learn in the workshop towards the further development of their communities by establishing community banks.

5. Methodology
An interactive workshop with a customised manual. Training will be in line with the principles of adult learning. Participants will be led to reflect upon their own experience. A case study approach will also be used.

6. Client to provide
Venue and refreshments as required, a suitably resourced conference room (including a data projector).

7. I am to provide
A manual for each participant and a notebook computer for use on the data projector.

8. Fee
For preparing and presenting the program: $2600 plus 10% GST = $2860. To indicate your acceptance, please pay a **deposit of $1100** (as described below).

9. Expenses
(a) Airfare, accommodation and transfers from Melbourne to Hobart and return. (Flights between Hobart and Melbourne are from $110

to $175 each way.) Allowing for one night's accommodation in Hobart, this item would cost between $450 and $650.)

(b) Travel from Hobart airport to the conference venue and return at cost.

(c) For each manual for each participant, $20 plus $2 GST for each workshop.

(d) Fees and expenses are payable within 14 days on receipt of invoice. Cancellation fee to apply in the event that the client cancels or changes the date of the workshop:

   (i) within three weeks of the event, 30 per cent of professional fee

   (ii) within two weeks of the event, 60 per cent of professional fee

   (iii) within one week of the event, 80 per cent of the professional fee.

(e) Any loss on fixed date air tickets or accommodation arising out of cancellation or deferral eight days prior to the event would be required to be made good by the client.

(f) All privacy and confidentiality requirements will be observed.

(g) John Treadgold to retain ownership and copyright of workshop materials and content for the aforesaid professional development activity prepared by him.

To accept this proposal, please authorise below. It shall remain current for 30 days. Thank you for the opportunity, we look forward to your response in due course.

Yours sincerely

John Treadgold

Principal Consultant

10. Acceptance

Should you wish to accept this offer, please convey your acceptance to johntreadgold@biglake.com.au and pay a **deposit of $1100** (including the professional fee at $1000 plus $100 GST) into our account at Westpac Bank 033 000 Account # 99 9999 in the name of Enterprise Community Consulting P/L ABN 78 000 000 000 or mail to the address in the footer of this letter.

(*Note:* As this is a conference which will depend on some funding, it may be that the organisation cannot pay you in advance. In that instance, you can request a letter of engagement or written advice from them that they want you to speak. Being a three-day conference and presumably one on a large scale, they will most likely have their own letter of engagement prepared by their own solicitors.)

11. Sample client list
A list of some of your relevant clients could appear here. Or you could list places that you have addressed as a speaker or trainer and organisations or communities that you have assisted to set up a community bank.

FOLLOWING UP

After you have sent the proposal you always telephone, normally twice. The first call is made the day after you send the proposal, just to make sure that they have received it.

The second call is made about one week after you sent it.

You ask, 'How did you find the proposal? Was it in line with your expectations?' As the second question is a closed one, inviting a short sentence response, you can ask the next question as an elaboration of that response. If the response was positive, you ask, 'What did you particularly like about it?' If the response is critical, you can ask, 'What were you expecting?' You can then clarify and change the proposal to suit.

Often the person you are dealing with will not be the real client but an intermediary. This can often lead to confusion, so it is in your best interests to find the real client. That is the person who benefits the most from your service and who has the authority to engage you and to access the resources that will be needed for you to do your work.

After you have had a number of meetings and lengthy discussions, you may like to hurry the decision-making along. You can say: 'Well, Rick (client), we've had extensive discussions. We've agreed on an approach (as you pat the proposal document). You've seen what I did at the other side of town, I'm sure that we can do it here at Performance Computers. If you were to go ahead, when would you want this done by?'

Rick says: 'Oh well, we will need that in place by the end of next month because that is when all the other signs come down. So that is in, let's see, about five weeks' time.'

You then say: 'Good. I could come in on Thursday week and attend to it then if you would like.'

They will either say: 'Okay, that will be good, thanks', or ask a question about fees or some aspect of the program or its delivery. If they already have someone else they will tell you or if they are interviewing others they will also let you know. You confirm your interest and then smooth over the conversation by asking some other question about their business. If you find this difficult you should consider undertaking some selling skills training, as the sale process will occur with every transaction you enter into. Often all you need to secure the sale is to agree to attend a client's premises on a certain date to do a defined task.

Other questions you can ask are:

- Tell me, is this in your business plan to do this year?
- Do you have budgetary approval to do this in the current financial year?
- If you were to go ahead, would you want this in both Sydney and Melbourne, or would it just be the Sydney office?
- Would you be proposing this for middle managers, or just the operations people?
- Would you want your delivery vehicles updated to be consistent with the new livery as well?

These questions are called 'trial closes' and lead you to ask further questions; you are almost taking an order for service delivery. If all goes well, they will say, 'Jenny, can you do this so that we will have it up and running within five weeks?'

QUIZ: WHICH IS THE CORRECT RESPONSE?

Response #1 'I'm pretty sure I can. Let me have a look at my diary here and . . . yes! I can start in ten days' time and that will see it all finished with two weeks to spare.'

Response #2 'Certainly can, Rick. How does tomorrow sound to you? We had better get on to this ASAP so we have plenty of time up our sleeves.'

Response #3 'I think I can, Rick. Let me go back to the office and have a look at my calendar and see how I am placed. I would certainly like to do it, it's just that I am very busy at the moment. There is a lot on.'

And the answer is: Response #3 is inappropriate, as you should not be seeking business that you cannot service. You should be able to commit if you are at the closing stage of the transaction. (I always carry my diary with me!)

Response #2 suggests that you have nothing else on. It is a little too urgent and it is doubtful that the client will be ready to go that soon.

Response #1 is measured, positive and you do have other clients who want you. Choose #1 and congratulations, you have secured the engagement!

Key points

- It is necessary to know how to secure the engagement because there are many competing demands on your prospect's attention and time.
- A quick read of Dale Carnegie's book, *How to Win Friends and Influence People*, is an excellent next step.
- Always be ready to take a business call. You never know when a referral or prospect is on the line.
- Research the prospect before you go to visit.
- Have an inventory of questions; develop a routine so that you find out as much relevant information as possible when visiting prospects.
- Often, to make the sale, all you have to do is to meet the client's request to be in a certain place at a certain time to perform a certain service.
- Be aware of what the benefits of your service are to clients and be able to articulate them.
- Be prepared to put your ideas and offers into written proposals.
- Know what questions to ask clients to help them come to a decision about proceeding with the project.

9
WRITING PROPOSALS

PROPOSALS: A CORE COMPETENCY!

In every relationship with a client, sooner or later something is going to be written. If you know the prospect and have a discussion with them, they will say, 'Send me a note about it, spell out what you want to do'. If your contact is not at the senior level in the organisation, they will say, 'Send me an outline of what you are proposing so I can show it to senior management'.

The proposal is your offer. An offer is one of the three components of a contract. The other two components are acceptance and consideration. In the absence of any other documents, the proposal will become the contract. If there is ever any lack of clarity about what the project was to be about, the parties would need to resort to the proposal document. 'In a dispute, the faintest line is stronger than the loudest word,' it is said.

So when practising as a consultant and endeavouring to win engagements, pay close attention to the writing of your proposals. The proposal is a marketing document, and the promise of what you will deliver. You will be judged twice: upon consideration for engagement, and upon delivery of your service. You need to get it right.

WRITING THE PROPOSAL

The proposal is what the consultant or freelancer sends to the client as an offer for an engagement. In the case of the contractor, the client normally issues a task description that the contractor is invited to perform. There may be exceptions to this practice from time to time but, if we stick to our original definitions, consultants and freelancers set the parameters while the contractor works within them.

The purpose of the proposal is to show your client what you will do for them. It will:

- demonstrate the benefit to the client of proceeding with the project;
- state the results (deliverables or outcome) that will be achieved;
- confirm the quality, timing and pricing aspects;
- clarify inclusions and exclusions;
- provide for variations to the brief once the project has started;
- provide for regular review once the project is underway; and
- in some instances, give the client options.

In most situations the proposal will also refer to the normal terms and conditions of trading. However, many larger organisations have standard contracts that they require consultants to sign. This is done as part of their own risk management procedures and for efficiency. Major corporations engage hundreds of service providers in any year and it does not make any sense for them to have their lawyers consider agreements drafted by all these service providers and their representatives.

A most important function of the proposal is that it provides the basis for the agreement between the consultant and the client. If the client signs the proposal, and the consultant advises the client that they have confirmed those dates in their diary and will proceed to prepare the project, there is a good argument for saying that the two parties have a contract. Even if the agreement is not signed, but there is some form of evidence that the client has agreed, some lawyers would argue that there is a contract in place.

A contract has three parts:

1. **The offer** That is your proposal.
2. **Acceptance** That is the client signature, although most clients in large organisations will not sign the proposal you send. They will say, 'Yes, that is fine. Let's set a date.' This is acceptance. You need to send an email confirming the phone call and putting whatever was agreed to in writing. For example:

   > Dear client. Thanks for your advice this afternoon that you have accepted the proposal dated 12 March whereby we shall review all your public documents and re-write them in plain English format. I have reserved those dates being 29 May to 29 June in my work program and will contact you at the start of May to arrange for the interviews of your three chosen stakeholders and for the delivery of the documents. I am looking forward to working with you. Thank you for the opportunity to provide my services.

3. **Consideration** That is making the days available, thereby saying 'No' to other clients who may have required you at that time. It may also include booking an airline ticket or purchasing special materials to conduct the assignment.

This form of operation is used by many consultants. If the client subsequently reneges on the arrangement and tries to avoid paying, then you need to be patient, assertive and go and see them if possible. You can also contact the company advocate within the organisation or the HR department. This way you will be dealing with someone who has extensive experience of dealing with consultants and who may be more sensitive to the reputation of the organisation.

It is good practice to stay in regular contact with a client once you have made an arrangement to be there in the future. This is to get the earliest possible advice of any changes to schedules so that you better manage the time risk.

GENERAL PRINCIPLES FOR WRITING PROPOSALS

1. **Use the client's language** If they talk about 'outcomes' or 'deliverables' and you normally say 'results', use their word but be sure you know what they mean by it.

2. **Avoid jargon** While jargon can be used to demonstrate that you have specific industry knowledge, it also has a number of disadvantages. First, it is generation specific. People of different ages usually use different jargon. Jargon is likely to be misunderstood and may lead to wrong outcomes. As it is also ambiguous, it may suggest that your diagnostic skills are lacking. Finally, senior management tends to be more involved with managing and less involved with the technical aspects of the business. They may not understand you and therefore award the work to someone else.

3. **Give options** You don't always know what the budget is, so offer the client the small, medium and large versions. Offer on-site and off-site delivery where appropriate. Let them choose for themselves whether they want the gold-plated version or the lean and purely functional version. Make sure that all the options have integrity. As a trainer I sometimes have clients who want a two-day program offered in half a day. If ever I was to accept such an engagement I am sure it would be a failure, as people in training programs can only move so fast. Better to say 'No' than to accept an undeliverable assignment.

4. **Use flow charts** Much of what consultants do is process work, and is often best described by use of a flow chart.

5. **Have a summary** Your covering letter should include a summary. To be able to see the key aspects of how much, when and what its special features are on one page may make your proposal more acceptable to the client.

A sample proposal for a short-term engagement is included on page 177. Here is a proposal for a longer term engagement.

LONGER TERM SAMPLE PROPOSAL
3 July 2007

Ms Elizabeth Fazio
General Manager
Bayside Catering Pty Ltd
58 Beach Boulevard
Port Melbourne Vic 3206
elizabeth.fazio@baycater.com.au

Dear Elizabeth
Business Review
It was good to meet with you on Monday and to hear about your business and network.

Here is the proposal that addresses the issues you raised. Please consider it and we can then discuss it as you see appropriate.

1. Introduction
Bayside Catering Pty Ltd (BC) is owned and managed by Elizabeth Fazio in Port Melbourne. It provides catering to a range of corporate, institutional and sporting organisation clients.

BC has 25 employees, of whom five are full time. Ms Fazio is aware that significant changes in the marketplace in terms of consumer preferences are taking place. Turnover has fallen in each of the past two years and three major clients have been lost with no significant new clients. Ms Fazio is reviewing the whole performance of the company and as part of this review is considering menu design and food preparation and presentation.

A full description of services offered by BC is listed at http://www.baycater.com.au.

Julie Cavallaro is a specialist adviser to the catering and food industry.

2. Service
In conjunction with Elizabeth Fazio, to review the current offerings of BC, to recommend a range of menus suitable for its clients and the

target market, and to give advice on food preparation and presentation, to train staff and to market the new menus and services so that the turnover, profitability and prosperity of BC is improved.

3. Objectives and deliverables
To improve the business performance of BC so that it may continue the excellent growth path of the previous five years where business grew at an average rate of 15 per cent in real terms.

Specific deliverables include:

(a) An Interim Report will be delivered at the completion of Stage 1 containing comment on the range of offerings, menu advice and sample menus, advice on food preparation and presentation. (This may be viewed as modification of the existing Business Plan for your organisation.)

(b) Training programs with materials, manuals and reports to the client on the competence of staff.

(c) A Marketing Plan to promote the business.

(d) A short Second Report will be delivered at the completion of Stage 2 containing advice on the business's aspects of turnover and profitability. This will also be in the context of the existing Business Plan.

4. Timing
The project is anticipated to take eight weeks, commencing Monday 6 August 2007.

Stage 1.1:   Identification and survey of target market
Stage 1.2:   Menu choice
Stage 1.3:   Sourcing and pricing of supplies
Stage 1.4:   Report and review
Stage 2.1:   Training of staff in preparation of new food offerings
Stage 2.2:   Marketing of new menus
Stage 2.3:   Evaluation
Stage 2.4:   Modification and redesign of offerings
Stage 3:   Continuing evaluation should you require

5. Methodology

All work will be undertaken according to the standards of professionalism of the Australian Institute of Food and Nutrition Consultants. These standards are attached to the proposal.

In the management and delivery of this project I will need to interview people from the company and a sample of clients and potential clients. This is necessary to obtain views of the market about their preferences for various menu and food types. I will also need access to senior managers within your company to ascertain various policy and performance information.

Delivery of the training workshops will be in accordance with the principles of adult learning: relevant to their own experience, practical, interactive, reflection, discussion, and skills practice.

6. Resources

(a) Client to provide:

Access to relevant company information on sales, clients, processes and personnel. Access to clients of the company and to the General Manager for interview. A car parking space at the Port Melbourne offices and a private office within the company premises.

(b) Consultant to provide:

Survey techniques and intellectual property relevant to the assignment and reports as described above.

7. Professional fee

For undertaking the project as described, and for attending four briefing sessions with the client prior to commencement of the project and two after its conclusion:

Stage 1: $8800 including 10% GST.
Stage 2: $6930 including 10% GST.

(*Note to readers—not for inclusion in the proposal:* The consultant has estimated Stages 1 and 2 of this project to be 24 days' work, which averages three days work per week for eight weeks. Her daily rate for an SME in this industry is $700 plus $70 GST totalling $770.)

Stage 3: This can be undertaken on a fee for service basis.

(*Note to readers:* Or you can say on an hourly basis of $96 ($770 divided by 8), but this is not wise here as the client will focus on your hourly rate rather than the assistance she is receiving from the project.)

8. Expenses
(a) Reimbursement of all travel and parking expenses incurred in the performance of this consultancy.
(b) Design and production costs of menu production. These are budgeted to be not more than $1500, including GST. In the event that changes are made after the menus and other items for printing have been approved, and in the event that the budget exceeds $1500, then the client shall be liable for the additional expenses as invoiced by our recommended designer and printer, Port Printing.
(c) For each set of training notes which will be bound with a wire comb and acetate front, a fee of $33.00 per person which includes GST. Alternatively, we can provide you with a master manual four days prior to the training workshops for you to print for each partipant prior to the workshops.
(d) Fees and expenses are payable within 14 days on receipt of invoice.
   • The first invoice is attached to this offer and is payable on acceptance of this proposal.
   • The second invoice shall be delivered on 3 September 2007 and payable by 17 September 2007. It shall comprise the full fee for Stage 1 and one-quarter of Stage 2 fee, plus expenses incurred.
   • The third invoice shall be delivered on 17 September 2007 and payable by 1 October 2007. It shall comprise one-half of the full fee for Stage 2 plus expenses incurred.
   • The final invoice shall be delivered on 15 October 2007 and payable by 29 October 2007 and shall be for the balance of the fee plus expenses.
   • Any delay to the implementation of the program shall not affect these dates unless agreed to in writing by both parties.
   • Any extension of the program shall be documented and invoiced at an hourly rate as agreed in writing by both parties.

(e) Cancellation fee to apply in the event that the client cancels or changes the date of the project commencement from Monday 4 August 2007. (*Note to readers:* This gives you negotiating room. Deferrals may be welcome to you.)

   (i) within three weeks of the event, 30 per cent of professional fee

   (ii) within two weeks of the event, 60 per cent of professional fee

   (iii) within one week of the event, 80 per cent of professional fee.

   Project expenses already incurred will be the responsibility of the client.

(f) All privacy and confidentiality requirements will be observed.

(g) Julie Cavallaro to retain ownership and copyright of workshop materials but gives licence to Bayside Catering to use them for the purposes of this consultancy.

9. Liability

This offer dated 3 July 2007 is for the purpose described herein and is solely and exclusively for Bayside Catering P/L. No liability is extended for any other use or to any other party.

   Further, while the advice we shall give is derived in part from our knowledge and expertise, it is based on the conditions prevailing at the time of the report and upon the information provided by the client and the client's associates at that time and which shall be summarised in the reports we shall present to the client as part of the project.

Note: You will need a clause to cover your liability for the provision of your services. It will need to be drafted by a lawyer who practises in the area of commercial law in the state or jurisdiction in which you offer your services and who does so in the light of knowledge about what it is that you offer and the circumstances in which you offer it.

   Some consultants seek to limit their liability to the extent of their professional indemnity insurance cover, as discussed on page 99.

To accept this proposal, please authorise below. It shall remain current for 30 days. We look forward to your response in due course.

Thank you for the opportunity.

Yours sincerely
Julie Cavallaro
Senior Consultant
M 0419 593 167

10. Acceptance
Should you wish to accept this offer, please convey your acceptance to julie@jcc.com.au and pay one-quarter of the professional fee of Stage 1 at $2000 plus $200 GST, a total of **2200**, into our account at the National Bank 999 999 Account # 99 9999 in the name of Julie Cavallaro Consulting P/L, ABN 99 999 999 999, or mail to the address in the footer of this letter.[1]

11. Sample client list
Once you have established a track record you can generally name the organisations you have provided services to, although the details of the services should not be disclosed without client consent. Disclosure is generally more acceptable to clients if the work is not of a strategic nature.

12. Terms
(Most clients will give you their own and so you will not have to draft it. Here is a summary of what is generally raised. Be careful what you agree to. If you are about to enter a contract that will pay you a substantial part of your income, my advice to you is to show it to a commercial lawyer. $500 is not much out of a $50 000 contract.)

- Fees & terms of payment   See above in the proposal Elizabeth Fazio.
- Termination clause   By either party on 30 (thirty) days' notice in writing to their registered office or registered place of business.

- Cancellation provisions — Through negligence or other security or performance aspects.
- Suspension — Perhaps for non-payment of moneys owed, or work not performed, milestones not met.
- Dispute resolution clause — In the event of a dispute arising out of this agreement, and the parties being unable to resolve it, they shall first use the dispute mediation services provided by the Law Institute of Victoria, or the Australian Food and Hospitality Council Ltd, whichever the client prefers.[2]
- No Partnership or Agency clause — Meaning the relationship excludes these aspects.
- Facility to provide for variations — Necessary—so that you can be paid for them.
- Confidentiality — Both parties shall respect the information they learn about the other's clients and activities and shall not use such information to the commercial or other disadvantage of the other party.
- Quotation validity — By you for a certain period of time, or to a certain organisation only.
- Liability — Who is liable for what. Many consultants seek to limit this. If there is PI insurance it is common to seek to limit the extent of the cover. Check with insurers as this may invalidate the insurance.
- Copyright — The author owns copyright unless the author is an employee or unless the contract requires that the consultant pass it to the client. Government contracts generally require this transfer. A normal compromise is to license the client to use it for the purposes of the relevant project.

- Protection/ownership of intellectual property

See an IP lawyer for your specific needs—copyright, trademarks, patents.

- Substitution clause

The client requires that the consultant conduct the work in the project. However, the consultant shall have the right to substitute another consultant who shall have similar skills, qualifications and capacity to himself, but that such substitution shall be subject to the client's consent and that such consent shall not be unreasonably withheld. (This is a substitution clause.)

CAUTIONARY FOOTER FOR EMAILS

The proposal often contains confidential information about the business practices of your prospects and clients. You should therefore have a note, such as the one that follows, in the event of a mishap occurring and the proposal falling into the wrong hands.

CAUTION—This message may contain information that is confidential and privileged intended only for the use of the addressee named above. If you are not the intended recipient of this message you are hereby notified that any use, dissemination, distribution or copying of this message is strictly prohibited.

If you have received this message in error please notify _____ (*me/you*) immediately by telephone number (07) 3333 3333 and destroy the message. Thank you.

Key points

- In every client relationship there will come a time when you need to put something in writing.
- A written summary of your work arrangements diminishes the likelihood of disputes about the scope, fees, terms, quality or any other issue.
- In proposals, make clear the deliverables or outcome, assistance and access you require, and any exclusions as well as inclusions.
- Use the language and terms the client uses.
- Avoid the use of jargon.
- Give the client options. They may not reveal all their needs nor all their constraints.
- Make your proposal readable. Use flow charts if appropriate, colour, and wider than standard spacing in your written work.
- Have a summary letter highlighting key points.

10
SERVICE DELIVERY

. . . always do more than what you get paid for. It's an investment in your future.

Jim Rohn[1]

THE ADVISORY PROCESS

Many consultants follow this process intuitively, but having some formal knowledge of the steps in consulting helps you do the job to match or exceed client expectations. It is well documented by Peter Block, and I have added the first step. It is important to complete each step or phase, otherwise it is quite likely that the client will feel that you have let them down.

1. RESEARCH THE CLIENT

There have been occasions when I have found myself dressing hurriedly in my business attire, racing out to the car and driving to meet a client at their premises. On the way I think to myself, 'Why didn't I look at their website?' You know so much more about a client when you check them out on the web. If the lead is from a referral then it is valuable to go to that source to profile the client.

Find out about the organisation and about its strengths and weaknesses. Sometimes an organisation may have had recent publicity, which might have been favourable or adverse. You will also develop a feeling about the job. Find out about the person, find out about the organisation and find out about the industry.

2. ENTRY AND PARTNERSHIP

In this phase you and the client determine whether you will engage in some form of project. If it is apparent that the client has a need, about which he or she will have varying degrees of awareness, during this stage you interview them to ascertain the current situation and where they would like to be. This can be viewed as a form of gap analysis, but in a relatively superficial form.[2] The need is established and a form of partnership is forged.

The partnership is critical, for if the project is to be successful the client needs to have some ownership. If you do everything, the client will be unlikely to have any sense of ownership of the outcome delivered. If any problems surface after delivery in such a case, it is likely that the client will simply blame you and perhaps not fix the problem.

If a partnership has been established, it is more likely that the solution devised by the consultant will have been customised to suit the client, and that the client's people will see it as their own creation and have a vested interest in keeping it running. They will see it through the teething stages. In the future, the client will be more inclined to get you back when they have a new project.

Following your initial meeting with the client, it is normal for you to submit a proposal and subsequently seek the client's reaction. (In contracting, the client will usually provide the document that is the work program or task specification.) For a relatively brief project, the proposal will be modified in accordance with the client's feedback and the client will consent by authorising the proposal. More complex projects require more meetings and more time to design.

It is always best that the proposal is put forward in writing and that you get the client's written agreement. If the client's consent is not in writing, then you should send a confirmatory email or letter to the client noting their consent and the details of how it was given.

3. ASSESSMENT

This is where you go into the organisation and conduct a diagnosis to more clearly establish the 'Now' situation. The diagnostic skills and methodologies you use will be appropriate for your professional area and competency. You do a detailed study of the current situation to determine the cause of the problem or to identify how the processes, product or business of the organisation can be improved.

The American consultant Peter Block suggests that you always conduct your analysis at three levels. The first level is what the client tells you: this is the 'apparent problem'. The second level is what the people who work for the client tell you, and this may be the 'underlying problem'. The third level is what you find out for yourself, and if your diagnosis is accurate; this should be the 'real problem'.

4. REVIEW AND DECISION

Having completed your assessment, you then work out what to report to the client and what recommendations to make. Sometimes this will be totally in line with what was thought likely in the initial meeting with the client. At others your recommendations may be quite divergent and require a greater allocation of the client's resources than was anticipated. As the final part of this stage, the client will decide either to proceed in line with your plan, or to amend the plan or to go no further. The client may wish to work with someone else. You can expect to experience all of these outcomes in your consulting career.

5. IMPLEMENTATION

This is the main part of the project. The engineer may build the bridge, the web designer creates a website, the HR practitioner introduces a performance appraisal system which involves a study of the existing system, creation of a new system, writing a manual, training personnel, observing the operation of the system and giving feedback to all participants. There may be continual design and development as various options are trialled. To this extent, the diagnostic activities of the phase three assessment continue. It may sometimes happen that the earlier work of the consultant or freelancer is so precise that another person does the implementation. Perhaps this person is a contractor.

6. MEASUREMENT AND EVALUATION

The project having been completed, it is assessed according to previously agreed evaluation criteria. Sometimes the client will have their own criteria or independent assessors to evaluate the success of the project. That would normally be made clear in the initial agreement. Measurement and evaluation is a continuing process and to some extent occurs throughout the implementation phase, as often the original needs change and the brief also changes. This 'brief creep' is a common phenomenon.

At the end, the client may want you to undertake the next step, whatever that may be. Alternatively, you may do the same project again on a different site or with different processes or people. It is also often appropriate for the project to finish and for you to go elsewhere.

HOW DO I HANDLE THE POST-DELIVERY PART?

During delivery you will have seen other opportunities where you could help the client. In the debrief or final review of the project, it is best to confine your remarks to the immediate project. You can make one reference to the fact that there are other matters where some improvements may be obtainable.

At an appropriate interval after the completion of the project, contact the client to 'see how things are going'. Suggest that you get together for a chat; that will be the time to bring up other issues. At this time it is likely that you will be more confident, more comfortable and more convincing.

Key points

In doing advisory work, make sure you attend to the six steps of the advisory process:

- Research the client. Find out as much as possible to enhance the prospect of knowing what they want and making delivery effective. It will also help you determine whether you actually want the job.
- Entry and partnership. Endeavour to attend to aspects of your dealings with the client that relate to non-technical matters. Building this relationship, and securing the client's participation and commitment to your project, is more likely to lead to the project's acceptance and success.
- Assessment. Ask lots of questions and realise that there are always three layers of information: what the client tells you, what the people who work for the client tell you, and what you find out for yourself.
- Review and decision. Process your information and work out, with the client, what you will do next.
- Implementation. Do it, review it, amend it, continue with delivery.
- Measurement and evaluation. See how effective your work has been. Take the opportunity to discuss the next step.

11
GROWING YOUR BUSINESS

THE FIVE AREAS FOR GROWTH

In this penultimate chapter we look to the future. Your business is running well. You have a clearly defined range of services, a small and growing client base and you are enjoying working from your own office, wherever it may be. By this time you will be aware of a number of issues that constantly arise. These issues relate to growth.

1. **Professional growth** The higher the profile you have adopted, the more it is expected of you that you will be at the cutting edge. How do you continue your professional development?
2. **Growth of your client base** Some clients will only have one project, others may use other suppliers and only use you occasionally when those others are unavailable. Some will leave their businesses, either by taking a new job elsewhere or selling their business to someone else. There are many reasons why clients move on. You will need to conduct a planned marketing campaign over a continuous period to provide new clients and perhaps to move your business towards clients that you come to prefer, perhaps because they will pay more.
3. **Growth in premises** Another issue related to growth will be whether to leave your lower-cost first office, which is probably at

home, to move into a larger commercial office. Such a move will probably require that you sign a lease for a minimum of six months, but possibly for three years.

4. **Growth through extra work** You may also consider taking on more work. At times you'll be offered more than you can handle. You could accept this work if you had employees or associates whom you could engage on a part-time basis.

5. **Growth through associations** Taking on bigger projects which require skill sets beyond your existing competencies has appeal to many service providers. This raises the issue of whether to go into joint ventures with other consulting firms.

While everyone will need to take on the first two issues, the others are moving away from the concept of a self-employed sole operator towards an entrepreneur and business manager. You will become a manager (again), with staff reporting to you, compliance rules in abundance and loss of flexibility. However, the financial rewards will often be there for the taking and the challenge, for some, will be irresistible.

By choice, and happily so, I work from a home office and have no employees but use the services of an accountant, a contracting book-keeper, a computer consultant and contractor, a designer and other service providers on a needs basis. In order to help you make decisions in these matters, I have sought the views of other consultants, free-lancers and contractors who have taken the path of growing their business beyond the sole operator stage. Their responses are included in the relevant sections below.

1. HOW DO I KEEP UP TO DATE?

Ideas are abundant in the corporate workplace, with trained and ex-perienced people working continuously on interesting and challenging projects. Where do you get ideas from in your solo environment?

One of the major challenges in working solo and possibly from home is that you now have to organise and pay for your own pro-fessional development. There are no similarly skilled professionals working in the room next to yours and you don't have as much published information available to you free—you now have to pay for subscriptions to professional associations, journals, newspapers and magazines.

The suggestions below have been found to work extremely well in providing for professional development. See how you find them.

JOIN INDUSTRY GROUPS AND PROFESSIONAL BODY NETWORKS

In Chapter 7 I recommended that you use these bodies as a primary marketing strategy. You can also use them for your own professional development. This will keep you in the loop as far as developments in your region are concerned. Your professional development will be catered for by the association, and you will build and sustain your network of personal links with others in the industry. This includes potential clients, former colleagues and other service providers.

You may like to take a position of responsibility. This will enhance your profile: the market participants will know you exist and that you are in business to serve them. You will be in a position to offer to chair sessions at meetings or conferences. You can influence agendas and gain speaking or writing roles.

The Australian Institute of Management conducts many meetings during any month covering a wide range of topics. In addition to audiences, they also need speakers and chairpersons. Someone is waiting for you!

SET UP A PEER MENTOR GROUP

When I first became a consultant, I was an inaugural member of a peer mentor group with people in a situation similar to my own. This is how it happened.

THE RECIPROCITY GROUP

My friend Alistair McArthur set up a group of six consultants new to business with the idea that we would meet to share information, to reciprocate, to 'barter PD', you might say.

Our meetings were held on the first Tuesday night of the month when hotels or restaurants would readily make a room available. The agenda for each month was 'Bring a problem or bring a solution'. Each person had to prepare a short paper (one page of A4) featuring the key points of their problem or solution. Sometimes the problem was simply a question, with the constraints written after the question.

In the early stages the kinds of issues discussed were:

- types of business structure: sole trader, partnership or company
- furnishing the business office: what is essential and where to buy it
- learning about and utilising our computers
- gaining new clients—marketing issues predominated
- compliance aspects: tax, workers' compensation and other insurances.

The position of chairperson was rotated and we could invite a guest or two, providing the group was no larger than ten. We found that once numbers were higher than this the group lost its focus.

The chairperson's role was critical to the success of the group. A total of twenty minutes was allocated to each participant: seven minutes to speak to their issue, the balance for discussion. No extension of time was allowed unless we had a very small number that month, as every issue was interesting and important to its sponsor. Sometimes we shortened the discussion if there was duplication of an earlier matter. While this sounds highly structured, it had evolved as the best system to ensure that we all contributed and all had the opportunity to learn.

Our members had diverse interests and no one was regarded as a direct competitor. The original group comprised the founder, Alistair, a risk management consultant focusing on the education and local government sectors; Kathy: outdoor adventure experiences for corporates, schools and other organisations; Diana: a promoter of jazz music and jazz musicians; David: a management consultant to agribusiness; Will: a project manager in the information technology area; and myself, the business skills training consultant. There were some changes over time as new members were added.

The group ran for twelve years. It had served us well but in its latter years became more of a social gathering than a cutting-edge or problem-solving forum. Perhaps it needed a higher changeover rate of membership. We always had people wanting to join, but it was sometimes difficult to reach consensus as to who should be admitted. As I write this I feel nostalgia for many happy times, lots of laughs and a lot of good ideas. It set out to be a forum for self-help in professional matters, but its members have become friends and confidants in a much broader and deeper way as our solo businesses have developed. It is sixteen years since we formed the group and with the exception of Will, who is now a horticulturist growing peonies, we are all still consulting.

You could set up such a group too. What makes it work? Trust, no competitors within the group, confidentiality, and commitment to preparing an interesting paper each month. The timekeeping helps too!

DO MORE INDEPENDENT RESEARCH

Use the Internet in addition to the newsletters, magazines, journals, research papers and newspapers you read.

Public libraries are another good source of regular, low-cost, up-to-date information. My local library has sunny open spaces, free Internet monitors and friendly staff who are prepared to help you with research. I can have a coffee and read the latest *Harvard Business Review* while the librarians look up and provide a list of what my American and German fellow practitioners are doing!

Undertaking your own research is also an effective way of combining professional self-development with marketing activity. You can use the research as a marketing tool as well as adding to your store of knowledge and expertise.

As a speaker and session presenter at conferences, I have often negotiated a free subscription to the whole of the conference. It's great for networking and for PD.

REBUILDING A PROFILE

Francis, a human resources practitioner, was offered and accepted an appealing position with a UN agency to work in Fiji for two years. He liked it so much that after a catch-up visit to family and friends in Sydney, he took up the offer of an additional two years.

Returning to Sydney, Francis set out to rebuild his profile, which had all but dissipated in the previous four years. He designed a questionnaire on issues relating to the conduct and interpretation of performance appraisals and sent it to 50 firms in his target market. These were organisations with more than 1000 employees. He then collated and interpreted the results and published a paper on 'Issues in the effective conduct of perform-ance appraisals'. He was also able to see how each firm differed from the norms and from his ideal type, or 'best practice' model.

Francis sent a summary of his paper to each of the 50 firms, asking if they would like to discuss the issue. This project created sufficient interest for Francis to resume his previously prosperous consultancy.

LEARN IT ON THE JOB

Most jobs involve something old, something new and, perhaps, something borrowed. What would you do if you faced the position shown in this diagram?

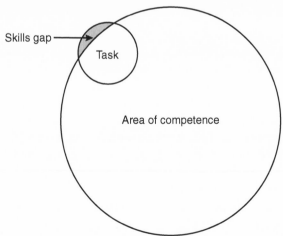

The large circle represents the consultant's area of competence. The smaller circle shows the client's needs. It can be seen that the consultant can meet 95 per cent of the client's needs. What does the consultant do about the shaded area outside their area of competence?

The consultant has three options: turn the project down, do it entirely alone or, third, do it as a joint venture with another party who will deliver the 5 per cent outside your area of competence.

Will you take this job? Should you say 'No' to the client? After all, the skill shortfall is minimal. I would be inclined to take it and then do one of two things depending upon when the service had to be delivered. If it is next week, the answer is to 'sub the task'—find another provider who can do that small portion while you do the rest. If the job starts in, say, ten weeks' time, then presumably you have the time to swot up, learn, practise and then deliver it yourself.

This situation is quite normal for the consultant. It is also normal for employees. We all learn on the job. As consultants you do need to grasp these opportunities, while not saying 'Yes' to everything that comes your way.

2. HOW DO I GROW MY CLIENT BASE?

Chapter 7 discusses the key aspects for growing your business. The concept of the client ladder is also valuable in understanding what your marketing processes are doing.

This is a very practical way to look at your marketplace. Your market participants are classified into one of five categories and placed on the appropriate rung of the ladder. Your marketing then involves identifying people on the ladder and taking action which will see them move up the ladder to a position of higher value to your business.

As you move your market participants up the ladder, your business will prosper. Marketing is much more costly on the lower levels and the cost of obtaining an engagement reduces as you climb the ladder. You tailor your marketing activities to meet the needs of individuals where they sit on the ladder. Clearly, the process of converting someone whom you already know from a first-time purchaser (customer) to a repeat-business client is different from attracting a new customer in the first place.

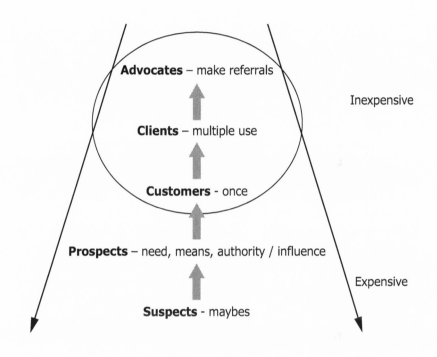

The ladder demonstrates that the most valuable person is the advocate, the person who refers clients to you. Advocates effectively do the marketing for you and therefore need to be kept aware of what you do, thanked for making the referrals and communicated with regularly. Advocates in business are most often former clients, past employers and parallel providers, people who provide complementary but different services. Examples of this might include a print shop business that acts as an advocate for a freelance copywriter, the computer supplier who refers the IT contractor and the lawyer who refers the independent counsellor.

Once a person is classified as a prospect, you need to make them aware of offers of services that you anticipate will arouse their interest. This is when you adopt and implement a relationship marketing strategy.

RELATIONSHIP MARKETING

If we ask consultants who have been in business for some years (ranging from carpet cleaners to dentists, plumbers and lawyers) where they get their clients from, they will usually answer 'by word of mouth, from people who know me'. This kind of response often makes new or prospective freelancers feel despondent, when they do not yet have an established pattern of clientele. If they develop a relationship marketing program, however, in time they will reap the benefits in the form of referrals and engagements.

The first principle of relationship marketing is getting close to people. There needs to be a strong personal element in the relationship. If your business is one which is primarily about you, in that you have no employees, then your name needs to be featured prominently on the letterhead and in all your marketing materials. Further, you need to spend time with the customer face to face and on the telephone. You can have a drink or a coffee with them, invite them to go somewhere with you and generally be available for discussion. It is best if you know what their personal circumstances are so you can talk about the people and issues in their life rather than just technical business issues.

A relationship with a client may follow when you get close to them. This will not occur with all or even a majority of the people you meet in business, but when their values are similar to your own, you understand one another, and goodwill and trust have developed the relationship is worth nurturing. It will become similar to the relationships you have had with friends and work colleagues.

A second principle, which is closely related to the first, is the need to put in, that is, being helpful and a source of utility to the other person. Over time, you can demonstrate expertise and knowledge and hopefully earn the trust of those people in the marketplace. Sooner or later someone will reciprocate by making a referral and you will be invited to attend a potential client's premises for an interview.

A third key principle involves the need to stay in touch, at least once every 90 days. This is best when it is done in a way that the client perceives as useful and perhaps helpful. Under such conditions your overtures will be welcome.

The overtures need to be continuous. One approach is rarely sufficient. It may take one or two years for some prospects to respond. This is quite normal, as everyone has their own priorities, and they may not see what you offer as meeting one of their current needs. Someone else may already be servicing them and, while they have an interest in your offerings, the other provider can get the go-ahead as a result of your promotional activities.

Continuous communication can be achieved by sending the client information in various ways: a copy of an interesting article you have come across; a newsletter relating to their job rather than information about what you are doing and offering; a reference to some event or activity or website that they can follow up. In all likelihood all these things will be of great interest to them; they will remind the client that you are thinking of them, that it is useful for them to know you and that you can help them achieve their business objectives.

RECIPROCITY

I often invite my best clients to lunch. I remember one such day in Hardware Lane in Melbourne, a pedestrian precinct featuring about 100 umbrellas and 500 tables on the cobbled pavement. The sun shines down into this north–south ribbon of a street for two to four hours, depending on the time of the year and the clemency of Melbourne's weather.

After we ordered our pasta my client said, 'I was just thinking about you the other day.' He went on to tell me of the plans at his organisation and where there was a role (not an opportunity, but a role!) for me. Later on he brought out a sheet, part of a proposal from someone offering a program similar to one I offered through his organisation. He asked me to look at point 6c. That, he said, was a good idea and how about I give some thought to incorporating it into my program.

I duly assented and we continued our lunch.

This has happened on numerous occasions. Clients invariably say, 'I was thinking about you just the other day . . .'. They will come up with opportunities for you and they will promote your interests!

This same man has said to me before that of all the consultants he deals with, he trusts me. He says I have helped him by making referrals and by doing things differently to accommodate his circumstances.

This relationship is now seven years old. We generally take it in turns to buy lunch. The bill is usually less than $30.

It is not every client that you take to lunch. It is the people you would be close to if you worked together, who you get on with. What you need to do is take the time to get to know a client as a person, to take an interest in them and to see how you can help them. They will respond and do the same for you. This makes it easier for both of us to get the result we want.

RELATIONSHIP MARKETING TACTICS

- Exceeding client expectations when you are engaged to deliver services. Arguably this is a necessary condition, as the client will need to be very pleased with your first service delivery if there is to be a chance of a second.
- Networking: relating, helping and doing so consistently over a reasonable period.
- Getting together for a chat is where you get to know your client as a person. This is an essential element of relationship marketing. Sooner or later you need to do this over the dining or coffee table. Most cultures have rituals based on dining. Eating together is special and it is personal. You should pay at first; if the relationship develops, ultimately they will return the hospitality.
- Telephoning—staying in touch from time to time. This is good to do at the end of the day or perhaps when there has been some event affecting the industry that everyone wants to talk about. Always ask the client, 'Are you okay to talk right now?' Your call will interrupt them and, while you have been planning the conversation, they may need to settle or perhaps suggest another time.

- Sending newsletters (with personal notes). Newsletters need to be interesting to the client so the content should help them. A newsletter about you is of no interest to your client base. A few words about yourself can be relevant though, just to make sure this tool conforms to the personal principle described above.
- Sending useful information. As a specialist you should continuously come across information and resources in which your client would be interested. Share these with your clients. They will underscore your expertise and your value to them.
- Giving referrals: treat your clients and prospects how you want to be treated.
- Attending seminars with prospects (or inviting clients to seminars as guests).
- Sending thank you notes. This is personal and highly individualistic if the note is well written.
- Sending appropriate greeting cards. If your client likes to display lots of Christmas cards, make sure you send one! If the client has no demonstrated interest in this form of correspondence, only send it if it is important to you to do so.

These same techniques are applied to customers, clients and advocates. In endeavouring to convert a customer to a client, it is important to exceed their expectations with your first engagement. This might be called giving added value. Many service providers proclaim that they provide value for money. This is a fairly minimalist claim, as most customers expect value for money and its mere provision means that expectations are not exceeded.

In summary, this system of personalised, continuous and helpful approaches is known as relationship marketing.

> All things being equal, people do business with friends. All things being not quite so equal, people still do business with friends. Make friends.
>
> Mark H. McCormack[1]

SO WHAT ABOUT DIRECT MARKETING?

Direct marketing relies on sending the target contact direct mail, using advertising and telemarketing. These activities are used early on to establish a base of prospects. You can also use it later when you decide to give your business a boost after a quiet time or when you have let your relationship marketing activity slip behind.

The tools of direct marketing are advertising, telemarketing, direct mail and websites. Some of these can be personalised but they tend to be shotgun in their approach at first, with later refinement as names of prospects emerge from a long list of suspects. The response rate to direct marketing tends to be very low. Wendy Evans suggests a response rate of 0.5 per cent as being average for a direct mail campaign—that is, one response for every 200 items sent out.[2]

Direct marketing activities tend to be costly as suitable marketing materials, such as brochures or flyers, need to be planned, designed and then printed. Marketing materials that are web-based will also need to be prepared by professionals if they are to stand out in the receiver's mail box.

Considerable time will need to be spent determining to whom these materials should be sent or mailed. If direct mail is used, the letters, labels, envelopes and flyers will need to be assembled. Mailing houses can be used, and databases can be purchased instead of doing this yourself, but the cost will run into thousands of dollars. It is for this reason that it is said that the costs of turning a customer into a client are much lower than the costs of turning a suspect into a prospect, or the latter into a customer. In other words, marketing activities for those on the higher rungs of the ladder are much less costly than activities directed at the bottom of the ladder.

Direct marketing tends to work better when it contains an identifiable offer, if it is special and if it is new. Many service providers tend to favour direct marketing methods as they are impersonal and take less of your personal energy and ego.

A SUCCESSFUL DIRECT MARKETING EXERCISE

Michael, a quality assurance consultant in Perth, wanted to build his profile in this area when it was new. He linked up with a well-known service club that had an ongoing 'Business in the Community' program. They agreed to jointly promote an introductory two-hour workshop on quality assurance.

A blue A4 brochure was prepared on standard 80 gsm paper. It was printed on both sides and folded into three as a DL document. (This meant that it folded down to fit into a normal business envelope.) The flyer gave details of the workshop, the fact that it was part of the service club's program and a few details on Michael, who would be presenting it.

This flyer was delivered to 4000 post office boxes in the South Perth region. The current cost of doing this would be about eight cents per letterbox. The seminar cost $45 to attend and eleven people took it up.

Michael was rewarded with two of the firms represented appointing him to conduct the ISO9000 accreditation process. The seminar led to him generating over $15 000 in revenue.

Four thousand brochures led to about 30 inquiries by phone (0.75 per cent response), eleven attendees (0.25 per cent acceptance) and then two engagements. These low response rates are typical of direct marketing programs but well worth the expense and effort. It was also far better than staying at home waiting for the phone to ring.

3. AM I READY TO MOVE INTO A COMMERCIAL OFFICE?

When you start in business, a good principle is to minimise recurrent expenses, those that occur regularly, every month or every quarter. The drain on finances that comes with the lease payments on a new car, new PC, new printer and new everything else in the office can be very depressing as you set out to convince new clients that they will benefit from engaging you.

As your business grows you will naturally contemplate whether you should have a 'proper' commercial office. If you decide to employ others or have clients come to your office, the external office will come to be seen as the answer to lots of the issues with which you are concerned.

Some of you will take commercial premises because there is no room at home or because home is too noisy. Others will do so as they see it as good business and good positioning to have the address and to be able to have clients attend at their office.

It is possible to have access to a serviced office for a smaller fee than having your own office. You can also rent the address, that is, advertise it as a mailing address. Such services are usually available for about $30 per month. There are inexpensive offices in the marketplace, usually one room in the office of another service provider. If you really need an external office, shop around. Look in the 'commercial premises to let' section of the Saturday newspapers.

I started out my life as a consultant in a commercial office. Six weeks later I was invited to join a merchant bank, with an offer too good to refuse, so I re-let the office and worked for the bank for almost three years, then very briefly as a director of a company which was about to be floated on the stock exchange. After an unpleasant month in this new position I resigned, and for the next year worked in the city with a major client, doing mainly contracting work as well as building my base of consulting clients.

Later, I took the opportunity to reoccupy these offices I had left over four years earlier. They were in my local shopping centre but the address was suitably commercial. For the next year I was rarely there, however, as I travelled to see my clients, many of whom were in other cities. The office became a millstone around my neck. It served no really useful purpose, and I had useable space at home. As our children were young, the formal dining room was rarely used and so it became my office. The home office has remained a successful and happy solution for me.

Prior to writing the first edition of this book in 2002, I surveyed ten consultants who have grown their businesses beyond the sole operator stage. One of them had over 200 consultants subscribing to his organisation from Australia, Britain and the USA. Another had up to

50 consultants working for him on a needs basis. The smallest is a group of two. I went back to them in 2007 for an update—my 2007 comments appear in italics.

These are their answers to my survey questions: Did you or do you work from home? If 'yes', did you ever have employees also working from your home? Could you comment on what issues were raised by that situation. What are the main (say three) issues to be dealt with when taking on commercial premises?

- **Jim** Yes. I am still in the garage; have avoided having an external office; away a lot; expense; it is another thing to manage. *I visited Jim's office in 2006—it is a high-tech purpose-built office attached to his garage. Jim has up to 200 consultants working for him on any day.*
- **Jeff** Yes, for the first two years. As space was small we separated admin support from professional work. Main issues are position relative to clients, layout and employee say in layout. *In 2007 this business is now a subsidiary of an American organisation and is run with commercial offices and staff in six centres near clients throughout Australia.*
- **Lyndal** We were in my mother's house but that became unmanageable. You do need to match premises with image you wish to project. My office is now in a separate house and this suits. *Canberra-based Lyndal has now merged with a Sydney-based firm and she has commercial offices in a suburb near the CBD. They are very big in the capitalisation of intellectual property and bio-technology.*
- **Andrew** Yes. I see no need at this stage for an external office as we visit clients at their premises. It does impact on home life, however. *In 2006, Andrew's firm was rated the 46th fastest-growing company in Australia by BRW magazine. They have commercial offices in Manuka, ACT.*
- **Chris** We started off in a colleague's house. There was a difficulty in meeting with clients but that can be managed. Ultimately we needed room for expansion; the location needs to be right and you may have special requirements to suit your purpose. *Chris has international success with his company and occupies specialist premises in a satellite suburb of Melbourne.*

- **Stephen** We started in commercial offices and then moved into home. We have contracted in size because two of our original partners moved out of the business. You need flexibility on the lease and good communication systems. *Stephen is doing extensive contract work with major banks and maintains both the home office with a virtual presence in St Kilda Road, Melbourne's equivalent of North Sydney, Spring Hill (Brisbane), North Adelaide and West Perth.*
- **Di** I work from home because it suits best. *It's on the Noosa River!*
- **Tam** I started that way but the bathrooms became too crowded. However, this was when the business was at its most profitable. Eventually we bought our own office as an investment. It is very costly to set up your office for specific business purposes, both in actual dollars and in terms of meeting cash flow requirements.[3] *Tam is prospering in New Farm (Brisbane) in his own offices and now has time for mid-week sailing on a regular basis.*
- **Jenifer** We work from home and we have offices. My partner (in life and in business) finds it distracting, but I like it. Key issues for offices are location, cost and lease flexibility. *Jenifer and Peter now have a team of twelve consultants based in a prominent commercial location in Canberra.*
- **Martin** I started in commercial offices. With young children, working at home was not an option. You need people around you: energy and interaction are creative forces. You also need to give yourself scope for growth. With offices, think about access to transport and parking. *Martin is thriving in his offices in Lane Cove, Sydney.*

4. DO I WANT TO TAKE ON STAFF?

The decision to take on staff involves you moving into a totally different area. You will need to have their day or week planned as well as your own. The best staff are self-managing but they still need constant communication with you so that they can self-manage effectively.

Martin's comment below is particularly instructive, *viz*: 'Once you take on staff you become a general manager and cease being a consultant.'

There are also myriad regulatory requirements relating to the employment of people.

I have had about five people work for me in my business. Working from a home otherwise empty during office hours, I have always engaged people known to me or well known to good friends of mine. This has been a form of protection against the potential instigation of unfair litigation. This is an aspect that none of my ten survey respondents raised.

If you decide to work with others, you are unlikely to suffer the loneliness which many independent consultants face. You can be energised by working with others and perhaps achieve some synergy. You are also in a stronger position in the marketplace because you have greater capacity and thereby a greater prospect of satisfying the client's needs. Your competitive position is enhanced.

The limitations of adopting a joint approach are mainly to do with the loss of independence for the consultant. Compromise and negotiation are a continual part of the process. Permanent partnership arrangements have additional complications as consultants are often involved in new and innovative fields which continually diverge. It is common to see two people who are united in year one doing quite different things in year three.

It is much easier to form joint ventures or partnerships on a project basis rather than on a continuous mode of operation basis.

My next survey question was: What three points would you make in hiring staff to work in your business? This is what my various respondents highlighted:

- **Jim** Thoroughness of selection, matching their aspirations. Need to ensure that these people bring or attract work in their own right.
- **Jeff** Reputation with client base. Understanding of where they want to be. Integrity of dealing.
- **Lyndal** Cash flow: make sure you can pay them. Seek a higher skill level so that they can contribute by both marketing and performing and by managing themselves.
- **Andrew** Need to contribute to income rather than be an overhead. Must be of a quality that you expect of yourself. Must have the interests of the business first and foremost in their minds.

- **Chris** Multiskilling, communication skills, and taking initiative.
- **Stephen** Presentation must be impeccable. Must have capacity for strong personal relationship building. Self-starting with staff management experience. Must be able to manage themselves in difficult situations.
- **Di** Need the skills and qualities you require. Customer focused. Share your approach. Doers and results orientated. Responsible and accountable for their own performance. Can both work autonomously and take directions.
- **Tam** Need to ensure that they are productive for every hour you pay them. Need an intense focus on billable hours. Cannot exceed time budgets. Must maintain the ethos: a client does business with you because they like your approach. You can lose a client if the new staffer has a different approach.
- **Jenifer** Staff must have their own network of potential clients and the drive and enthusiasm to market and to win business for themselves and for others. Be aware of the expected utilisation rate and the full cost of hiring staff. Staff must have the requisite skills, team approach and preferably shared values.
- **Martin** Recruitment is like a lottery, and you will make mistakes; don't worry about them. Don't rush, even when you really need someone. Think of ways to check out their claims about their skills. Once you take on staff you become a general manager and cease being a consultant.

5. AM I READY FOR PARTNERS?

Consultants are ideally placed to undertake projects on a joint-venture basis. Most projects require a combination of skill sets, and while the hirer may often put teams together there is a valid role for independent project managers to do so. That is effectively what my respondent, principal consultant and contractor Jim does. He now has a team of about 160 consultants whom he can draw on as the needs of client projects dictate.

The trend in business is for corporations to focus on their core activity and for anything else to be outsourced or contracted out to the lowest but competent bidder. This is also the case in consulting. Firms have a core staff who are specialists in the most common areas of client need—IT, HR and organisational behaviour and development, finance, and project management—and they access other specialists on a needs basis. These include legal, occupational health and safety, training, risk managers and many others.

My experience is that while I have developed longer term relationships with quite a number of clients, I have developed very few longer term relationships with other consultants, freelancers or contractors. One of the reasons is that my work tends to be of a short-term nature and is highly identified with me, so subbing it is not something that I wish to do and nor does the client want it done. Second, I tend to mix more with clients than I do with other consultants. However, the main reason I think is that while my strength is the ability to run my own show, my weakness is that I am not so good in a team. I like to take responsibility and having only myself to hold to account. I think this is one of the paradoxes in this business.

In response to the question, What in your view are the major issues to be dealt with in forming joint ventures with other service providers?, here is what my panel of experienced service providers thinks about forming joint ventures. Most of them do it regularly.

- **Jim** Check their integrity and business habits; scope and agree commercial expectations with them; keep in contact and check with client on progress.
- **Jeff** Shared end goal (not the stated one, the real one); similar culture and approach; work share.
- **Lyndal** Trust; subbies will not own the project; if they are true partners then they need to share the wins and the problems; legal aspects as to whether they are employees or partners; additional PI [professional indemnity] costs.
- **Andrew** Complementarities more important than overlap. Need a clear understanding of the relative contributions and of IP [intellectual property] issues.

- **Chris** Trust, greed and consistency of approach. Consultants are ambitious and often jealous of the principal's share—there is a need to understand that the principal has taken the risk.
- **Stephen** Need a good heads of agreement; ownership of the client to be clear; PI issues.
- **Di** Need to have a shared vision of the outcomes. Need to see that they actually do the work to your own high level and need to meet the deadlines set.
- **Tam** Always a difficulty; someone needs to take the lead; issues are profit share, egos and communication.
- **Jenifer** Relationships tend to be either mutual and long term or short term and opportunistic. Not always possible to determine until you have worked with each other. It is very disappointing when long-term ones finish prematurely.
- **Martin** I steer away from them.

It is very important to be aware of the issues to do with legal liability for the work undertaken. As the members of the partnership may have differing legal structures, it is best to consult an accountant or a commercial lawyer before formalising joint-venture arrangements.

Key points

- Develop your own professional development activities. Consider building your profile in your relevant industry or professional associations. Set up a peer mentor group or reciprocity group with like-minded service providers.
- Conduct a survey of your target market. You will find out what they need, and they will be interested to hear you say or to read what you write about it.
- Develop a relationship marketing strategy to stay in touch with the key people in your target market. Make sure you provide some useful form of contact every 90 days.
- Conduct some direct marketing activities from time to time to gain new prospects.
- If you move into commercial offices, look for flexibility on lease terms. Ask yourself: 'Are this location and this building consistent with how I wish to be regarded by the market?'
- When taking on staff, ensure that you have productive work for them to do, that you are capable of organising them and that you have consulted an expert about your legal and other liabilities.
- When doing joint ventures, discuss all relevant matters including the break-up of the arrangement, and clarify each party's responsibilities, liabilities, amount and terms of payment, and *always* document the agreement.

12
IT'S THERE FOR THE ASKING. DO YOU WANT IT?

If you have read this far I expect that you are well on your way to becoming a self-employed consultant. Irrespective of which of the five groups you spring from—passionate practitioner, lifestyle seeker, restructured recruit, reluctant recruit or business-building entrepreneur—interesting and rewarding experiences lie ahead.

In my capacity as a consultant, I have met many CEOs, CFOs, CIOs and government ministers. I have advised heads of our armed services and coached politicians and CFOs of corporations. I have advised well-known people on how to build profile as consultants.

ABC Radio, Qantas in-flight business, Open University and the National Press Club have featured me in their programs and I have contributed to many publications. I have been paid the ultimate accolade of being imitated and plagiarised!

There have been some hundreds of nights spent with clients and friends in wonderful places: in the Southern Highlands, Margaret River, the Murray River, Alice Springs, the Victorian high country, numerous wine districts and far north Queensland. There have been many hours at lunch with clients overlooking sensational water views in Sydney, Hong Kong, Salamanca Place and the New South Wales Central Coast.

In 1997 I was in Newcastle, three days after the closure of the BHP steel mills had been announced, conducting a pilot program for the departing engineers on how to set up as consultants and contractors. This led to twenty programs being presented over a three-year period.

One of the most rewarding aspects has been to work with the consulting firms and units now run by people who attended my training courses over five years ago. I enjoy the continuing personal and professional association with these people in contrast to much of my business, which is a bit more like the 'one night stand'—spend a day together, intimate discussion, then leave!

Every time I send out my newsletter I receive positive and encouraging emails from people I have helped in making their own businesses viable and in turning their lifestyle dreams into reality. On average five of the 2000 newsletters come back to me with invitations for engagements. That makes the effort worthwhile.

Most of the Australian cities are now well known to me. I am at home in all the capitals as well as in Singapore, Wellington and Christchurch. There is someone to have dinner or coffee with in each place.

These are some of the highlights of my career as a consultant. I commend it to you!

In closing, here are what my consultant associates variously see as the advantages of this lifestyle.

- **Jim** Satisfaction; wealth accumulation; independence.
- **Jeff** Helping improve client businesses; seeing our people grow; sense of purpose and achievement.
- **Lyndal** Independence; income; authority and profile.
- **Andrew** Control of own circumstances; good income—rewarded for own efforts; potential for growth into a field that is global.
- **Chris** Life balance; independence; pleasure from giving to others.
- **Stephen** Networking with many different people and from different organisations; lifestyle: do what I want, when I want, with the people I want; I am in control of my own destiny.
- **Di** Flexible hours and balanced lifestyle; autonomy and being my own boss; not getting involved in office and business politics.

- **Tam** Being your own boss—you live and die by the decisions which are yours; flexibility on how you use your time; financial opportunity to earn as much as you dare dependent on the opportunities and your ability.
- **Jenifer** Rewarding work which is very satisfying, helping clients achieve what they could not achieve on their own; good income; growing the business is satisfying.
- **Martin** Money, independence, esteem.

Three years ago I moved to the hinterland overlooking Maroochydore on Queensland's Sunshine Coast. The Queensland government departments give great support to small businesses, including consultants. I thought I would build my business in south-east Queensland but the main growth has been in Sydney. I am very happy with that although I am now looking to do something overseas. We'll see. Why don't you do your thing too?

ENDNOTES

Chapter 1

1 E. James Rohn, *The Treasury of Quotes*, Griffin Paperbacks, Netley SA, 1994, p. 56.

2 Peter Block, *Flawless Consulting*, 2nd edn, Jossey-Bass, San Francisco, 1999.

3 *Business Review Weekly*, 17–23 January 2002, p. 44.

4 Where individual contractors own extensive plant and equipment that they use on projects this assertion does not apply. Examples include harvesting contractors, engineers with special testing equipment and mining exploration specialists. Psychologists often pay rights to use special tests but these are most often on a fee-for-usage basis and the cost is passed directly to the client.

5 SMEs are small to medium enterprises with up to 50 employees. Micro businesses are those that employ fewer than five people. ABS statistics show that 88 per cent of small businesses in Australia are micro businesses.

Chapter 2

1 Cynthia D. Scott and Dennis T. Jaffe, *Managing Change at Work: Leading People Through Organisational Transitions*, rev. edn, Crisp Publications, Menlo Park CA, 1995, p. 33; see also J. Mahoney, 'Grief: a clinical model for healers', <http://www.jmahoney.com/Grief.html>.

2 Believed to be the work of John H. Howard but not confirmed.

Chapter 3

1 James Rohn, *The Treasury of Quotes*, Griffin Paperbacks, Netley SA, 1994, p. 83.

2 Attributed to Dwight D. Eisenhower by Patrick Anderson, *The Presidents' Men: White House Assistants of Franklin D. Roosevelt, Harry S. Truman, Dwight D. Eisenhower, John F. Kennedy and Lyndon B. Johnson*, Doubleday & Company Inc., Garden City, New York, 1968.

3 Rudyard Kipling, *The Elephant's Child*, from *Just So Stories: For Little Children*, Weathervane Books, New York, 1978, p. 66.

4 David H. Maister, *True Professionalism: The Courage to Care About Your People, Your Clients, and Your Career*, Free Press, New York, 1997.

Chapter 4

1 Australian Bureau of Statistics reported that at June 2000, a total 980 300 persons were classified as persons working from home. ABS 6275.0 Locations of work, Australia, <http://www.abs.gov.au/ausstats>, accessed 28 May 2001.

2 'Napping enhances worker productivity: scientific proof', in *Napping News* (from eFuse), <http://www.efuse.com/nap>.

3 Geoff Bellman, *The Consultant's Calling*, Jossey-Bass, San Francisco, 1990, p. 53.

4 Some reading or training in personality type is useful in understanding how people prefer to receive their information and in what interests them. It also gives insights into what annoys them. Two well-known techniques are the Myers Briggs Personality Type Indicators (MBTI); see Jan Noring, 'Personality type summary (Myers-Briggs)', 1993, <http://www.pendulum.org/misc/mb.htm>; Dr Stephen Moss, *Introducing Type: An Australian Handbook on Jungian Type Theory and the Myers–Briggs Type Indicator (MBTI)*, 3rd edn, DMP Publications, Brisbane, 1988; 'The DISC System', *DISC:Principles*, <http://www.discinterconsult.com/disc/princip.html>.

Chapter 6

1 Geoff Bellman, *The Consultant's Calling*, Jossey-Bass, San Francisco, 1990, p. 202.

Chapter 8

1 E. James Rohn, *The Treasury of Quotes*, Griffin Paperbacks, Netley SA, 1994, p. 71.

2   David Maister's writings are listed at <http://www.davidmaister.com>.

3   Dale Carnegie, *How to Win Friends and Influence People*, rev. edn, Angus & Robertson, Sydney, 1989 (first published 1936).

4   See Chapter 4, endnote 4.

Chapter 9

1   We cannot always negotiate a prepayment. However, some form of commitment from the client is highly desirable for such a big project.

2   In this instance the consultant is happy to use the relevant law society. There are many other organisations you could use. It may be better to keep it away from lawyers!

Chapter 10

1   E. James Rohn, *The Treasury of Quotes*, Griffin Paperbacks, Netley SA, 1994, p. 29.

2   The 'gap' in gap analysis is the gap between the current situation, the 'now', and the ideal situation, the 'where' the client would like to be.

Chapter 11

1   Mark H. McCormack, *What They Don't Teach You at Harvard Business School*, Collins, London, 1984.

2   Wendy Evans, *How to Get New Business in 90 Days and Keep It Forever*, Millennium Books, Sydney, 1993.

3   Prior to publication of the first edition, Tam went on: 'Last year we needed to expand the office to upgrade existing equipment and to engage three more people. So we spent $20 000 in May on computers, office furniture, software, etc. The cash out was $20 000 but the Taxation Office view this as an asset for depreciation for, say, two months, giving 2/12 of 20% depreciation allowance or $600 deduction on our tax return. The balance remains as profit so we pay tax on $19 400, at now 30c in the dollar or $5820. The actual cash that the business has spent is $25 820, all in an effort to expand and employ more people. Sure, over the next five years we get a deduction for the investment but that shows no understanding of the cash flows and the strains that it creates on small business. To self fund, expansion will always be limited by the Taxation Office in this way!'

RESOURCES

FOR BUSINESS SET-UP

Business Entry Point (BEP)

<http://www.business.gov.au>
BEP is a gateway that provides all government–business and business–government interactions online, regardless of level of government. It includes local, state, territory and Commonwealth governments, and several industry and business associations.

This site makes it easier to find government information, to complete compliance processes and to identify suitable support or assistance programs.

From the BEP site you can link to the Australian Business Register Online where you register online for an ABN, and also link to the online registration for GST.

This site will lead you to the following:

Australian Business Number ABN

<http://www.abr.business.gov.au>
Online registration for your ABN is done through the Australian Business Register Online <http://www.abr.business.gov.au> and can

also be accessed through the Business Entry Point <http://www. business.gov.au>. From this site you can simultaneously obtain a tax file number and register for GST online.

Goods and Services Tax GST

<http://www.ato.gov.au>
Follow the link to business on this site. You can register electronically direct at this address, through the Business Entry Point at <http://www.business.gov.au>, or send your completed application to the ATO. Your tax agent can also lodge your application through the Electronic Lodgement System.

Australian Taxation Office ATO

<http://www.ato.gov.au>
This site links to ATOassist–for Business and covers all the tax issues for starting a business. The site can be searched by keyword and by the A–Z of taxes and topics. Valuable information includes business structures, GST and superannuation. If you have a question on general income tax for business, ABN or PAYG legislative guidelines, you can email SmallBusinessLaw@ato.gov.au.

Tel 13 28 66

Australian Securities and Investment Commission ASIC

<http://www.asic.gov.au>
The ASIC site has many useful links, including to the ATO and the Business Entry Point. It gives information on starting a business, on companies and how to register them.

The *Corporations Act 2001* can be downloaded in PDF format from this site. ASIC also provides a number of free Internet searches of information lodged with it under the provisions of the *Corporations Act 2001*.

From here it is possible to search the **National Names Index** to find basic details about current and former companies, business names and other organisations. **Identical Names Check** can also be searched to check that the company name you are proposing is not identical to one already registered on the ASIC database.

ASIC has service centres for document lodgement and compliance inquiries in each capital city and in many regional centres throughout Australia.
Tel 1300 300 630

New Zealand
<http://www.govt.nz/services/>
Follow links to Starting a Business for information about the numerous forms of assistance.

BUSINESS NAMES AND OTHER STATE GOVERNMENT SERVICES
For information on business names, consult the first listing under the state entries below. Information about other government-sponsored activities, including networking and training, appear as the subsequent entries under these state headings.

Australian Capital Territory
<http://www.rgo.act.gov.au>
Registrar General's Office
255 Canberra Avenue, Fyshwick ACT 2609
Tel (02) 6207 0473

New South Wales
<http://www.fairtrading.nsw.gov.au>
Department of Fair Trading
1 Fitzwilliam Street, Parramatta NSW 2150
Tel 13 32 20

New South Wales Business Service Sector
<http://www.nsw.gov.au/Business.asp>
Business Service gives all relevant information for starting and operating your small business, licences, regulations, permits and business name.

Small business website

<http://www.smallbiz.nsw.gov.au>
Links to information for small business including the Small Business
Advisory Centres, resources, licences, regulations and permits.
Tel 13 11 45 in NSW; (02) 9338 6666 outside NSW

Northern Territory

<http://www.caba.nt.gov.au>
Consumer and Business Affairs
Development House, 76 The Esplanade, Darwin NT 0800
Tel (08) 8982 1700; 1800 193 111

Queensland

<http://www.consumer.qld.gov.au>
Office of Fair Trading
Level 21, State Law Building, 50 Ann Street, Brisbane Qld 4000
Tel 13 13 04

Queensland Government—Business and Industry: Smartlicence

<http://www.qld.gov.au/business_and_industry>
This site provides all the information needed for starting and operating
a business in Queensland, including business licences and registrations
and government regulations.
400 Boundary Street, Spring Hill Qld 4004
Tel 1300 363 711

South Australia

<http://www.ocba.sa.gov.au>
Business and Occupational Services
Ground Floor, Chesser House, 91–97 Grenfell Street, Adelaide SA 5000
Tel 13 18 82

The Business Channel

<http://www.southaustralia.biz/home_page.htm>
The Business Channel is a gateway to Business Entry Point, Centre for
Innovation, Business and Manufacturing, and Business Licensing.

Tasmania
<http://www.consumer.tas.gov.au/business_affairs>
Business Affairs
134 Macquarie Street, Hobart Tas 7000
Tel (03) 6233 4104

Victoria
<http://www.business.vic.gov.au>
Gives information and assistance for starting or growing your small business. This site provides information and referral services. It works with other government agencies and private sector small business service providers. There is a link from this site to Victoria's Business Licence Information Service.
113 Exhibition Street, Melbourne Vic 3000
Tel 13 22 15

Small Business Counselling Service
<http://www.sbcs.org.au>
A non-profit organisation providing 50 experienced volunteer counsellors for counselling and mentoring to medium, small and micro business in Victoria at a minimum cost.
Tel 13 22 15

Western Australia
<http://www.wa.gov.au/businessinwa/businesslink>
Department of Consumer & Employment Protection, Business Names Branch
219 St Georges Terrace, Perth WA 6000
Tel 1300 304 014

Small Business Development Corporation (SBDC)
<http://www.sbdc.com.au>
SBDC is a WA state government agency focused on the development of the small business sector; provides information and links to related sites.
553 Hay Street, Perth WA 6000
Tel 13 12 49

OTHER GOVERNMENT SITES

Australian Commonwealth Government Entry Point

<http://www.fed.gov.au>

This is a portal developed to provide comprehensive and integrated access across the Federal public sector from a single point. There is a link from the home page to <http://www.gov.au> that provides access to all state and territory governments.

Business Licence Information

<http://www.bli.net.au>

This site provides access to information on licensing requirements for business at all three levels of government—local, state and Commonwealth.

PROFESSIONAL ASSOCIATIONS AND INDUSTRY BODIES

Association of Professional Engineers, Scientists and Managers, Australia (APESMA)

<http://www.apesma.asn.au>

Provides extensive services for consultants including PI insurance and other insurances, and is a provider of professional development in most states.

163 Eastern Road, South Melbourne Vic 3205 and offices in all states

Tel 03 9695 8800

Australasian Facilitators' Network

<http://www.facilitators.net.au>

The Australasian Facilitators' Network (AFN) is a self-organising community of practitioners based in Australia, New Zealand, South-East Asia and the Pacific, who have been meeting since 1992. Bob Dick moderates a list server that members use to solve problems and share information. There is also an annual conference. This is an excellent source of ideas and skills development for one of the fundamental skills of consultants: facilitation.

Australian Institute of Company Directors (AICD)

<http://www.companydirectors.com.au>

Organises training in directorship: responsibilities, competence, governance and networking activities.

Level 2, 255 George Street, Sydney NSW 2000 and offices in all states.

Tel (02) 8248 6600

Australian Institute of Management (AIM)

<http://www.aim.com.au>

Organises many networking groups that are appropriate for consultants. The AIM is also a large provider of professional development.

Tel 13 16 48

ACCOUNTING BODIES

CPA Australia

<http://www.cpaaustralia.com.au>

Institute of Chartered Accountants of Australia (ICAA)

<http://www.icaa.org.au>

LAWYER BODIES

Can give referrals to appropriate commercial lawyers for advice on forming business ventures, including original set-up. Most provide professional development activities.

Law Institute of Victoria

<http://www.liv.asn.au>

Law Society of New South Wales

<http://www.lawsocnsw.asn.au>

Queensland Law Society
<http://www.qls.com.au>

The Law Society of South Australia
<http://www.lssa.asn.au>

The Law Society of Tasmania
<http://www.taslawsociety.asn.au>

The Law Society of Western Australia
<http://www.lawsocietywa.asn.au>

INSURANCE

Australian Securities and Investment Commission ASIC
<http://www.asic.gov.au>
All insurance agents and brokers in Australia must either hold an Australian Financial Services (AFS) licence or be an employee or authorised representative of a licence holder. Check this site for information.

PI insurance
Professional indemnity insurance is normally provided by your own professional body, or through insurance brokers. Try APESMA as well (see above) at <http://www.apesma.asn.au>.

Business insurance
Business insurance is provided by commercial companies including:
<http://www.suncorp.com.au> Suncorp Metway Group, tel 13 11 55
<http://www.nrma.com.au/pub/nrma/business/index.shtml> Insurance Australia Group, tel 13 28 18
<http://www.allianz.com.au> Allianz Australia Insurance Limited, tel 13 10 00

WORKPLACE INSURANCE

Victorian WorkCover Authority
<http://www.workcover.vic.gov.au>
Tel 1800 136 089

WorkCover Corporation of South Australia
<http://www.workcover.sa.gov.au>
Tel 13 18 55

WorkCover New South Wales
<http://www.workcover.nsw.gov.au>
Tel 13 10 50

WorkCover Queensland
<http://www.workcover.qld.gov.au>
Tel 1300 362 128

WorkCover Western Australia
<http://www.workcover.wa.gov.au>
Tel 1300 794 744

Workplace Standards Tasmania
<http://www.wsa.tas.gov.au>
Tel 1300 366 322

Accident Compensation Corporation NZ
<http://www.acc.co.nz>

BUSINESS ENTERPRISE CENTRES OF AUSTRALIA

Business Enterprise Centres (BEC) are located in city and country areas in some states to assist you in expanding your existing business or to explore new ideas. These include:

<http://www.bec.com.au> Business New England North West
<http://www.basi.com.au> Business Advisory Services Incorporated (BASI) in Parramatta.

OTHER RESOURCES FOR CONSULTANTS

Australian Copyright Council
<http://www.copyright.org.au>
Clarify copyright issues by accessing the documents and training opportunites available here.
Suite 3, 245 Chalmers Street, Redfern NSW 2016
Tel (02) 9318 1788

Ian Benjamin's site for consultants
<http://www.ianbenjamin.com.au>
Ian Benjamin is constantly training, speaking and writing for consultants, freelancers and contractors. His personal site will at times update the information in this book and lead you to other resources that can assist you in running your business.
Tel 0419 593 167

Consultant Training Australia Pty Ltd
<http://www.consultanttraining.com.au>
Provides training workshops, articles, newsletters, coaching and other services for consultants.
Tel 0419 593 167

<http://www.interchangepubs.com.au>
Bob Dick's excellent facilitation skills training and publications available here.

<http://www.businessballs.com>
Alan Chapman's generous website containing hundreds of free consulting tools.

<http://www.thiagi.com>
Innovative supplier of games for trainers and facilitators.

<http://www.flyingsolo.com.au>
Newsletters, articles and virtual networking.

<http://www.sbinformation.about.com>
Information on small business from the USA.

<http://www.businessknowhow.com>
Information for home offices, small business and careers in the USA.

<http://www.sbinfocanada.about.com>
Information for small business from Canada.
BUBL

<http://www.bubl.ac.uk>
Carefully selected Internet resources covering many subjects.

INDEX